TWENTY-ONE POSITIVE PRINCIPLES

FOR A POWERFUL

TWENTY-FIRST CENTURY CHURCH

Dennis A. Davis

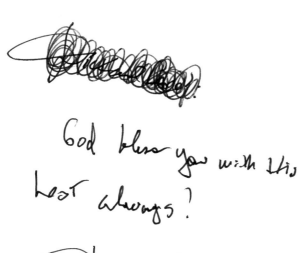

God bless you with His
heat always!

3 John 2

DEDICATION

To my wife, **Nancy**, my college sweetheart, who identified with my calling, has faithfully been my partner, my strongest supporter and greatest encouragement to my life and ministry.

CONTENTS

Contents

TWENTY-ONE POSITIVE PRINCIPLES

FOR A POWERFUL

TWENTY-FIRST CENTURY CHURCH!

FOREWORD

Having dedicated a life-time to the ministry and in building the Church of Jesus Christ, not just locally, but through the lives of ministers who have sought to discover the principles that guide growth and success, this becomes an important book for those who are serious in guiding the church through this Twenty-First Century.

Over thirty years ago, as I began the Robert Schuller Institute For Successful Church Leadership, I met a relatively young man at our first Institute by the name of Dennis Davis. I watched him as he left that Institute to go back to the church where he was pastoring and put those principles that we shared to work. I invited him back on several occasions to speak at the Institute to share his exciting story. He has been involved as my friend to this ministry now for over these thirty years, and is now serving with me on our pastoral team in the development of church leaders. He is one of those who took the principles that we share and put them into practice in building a great church. Through his own life experience he now has placed these principles in an intriguing format based on the Book of beginnings for the church, The Book of Acts in the New Testament.

If we are to see enduring growth and success in the

church, those principles that motivate us that we practice must be based on strong biblical foundations. These principles have been captured in this book.

—Robert H. Schuller

PREFACE

This book comes out of a lifetime of ministry. I now find myself, after forty-five years in the ministry, serving with Dr. Robert H. Schuller at the Crystal Cathedral in Garden Grove, California. What a privilege it is, recognizing that I am nearing the end of active ministry, to be associated with one of the three men who have most influenced my life and direction in ministry.

I was coming to the close of an eight-year tenure, serving as President of Northwest College in Kirkland, Washington and contemplating retirement. Out of the blue, totally unexpected, Dr. Schuller called one day and invited me to come serve with him as the Executive Director of Robert Schuller Ministry to Ministers. In 1970 I attended the first Robert Schuller Institute For Successful Church Leadership held on the campus of what was then called the Garden Grove Community Church. I had a life-changing experience in preparation for, and while attending the Institute. I was able to not only formulate a vision, but to put into a framework of guiding principles to see it accomplished. Kirbyjon Caldwell, the senior pastor of Windsor Village United Methodist Church in Houston, Texas, expressed my sentiments regarding the Institute when he said, "This Institute told me it was alright to think outside of the borders, outside of the box."

Life has been interesting for me. When I was a senior in high school I felt God's call upon my life to the ministry. Since that "call" I completed a four year baccalaureate degree in theology, served as a traveling evangelist for five years in my younger days, pastored twenty-six consecutive years (twenty years as senior pastor of The People's Church in Salem, Oregon), served as a District Superintendent, overseeing over 200 churches in Oregon, and then was asked to serve as the fourth president of Northwest College in Kirkland, Washington in 1990. (The college conferred an honorary doctorate degree upon me in 2002.) I have been privileged to speak and travel in 26 countries.

One of my desires is to be a life-long learner. At present I am finishing up a Master of Arts degree program at Vanguard University in Costa Mesa, California in Church Leadership.

My entire life has been involved in the church, with a particular interest in church growth. I am blessed by my heritage. My father was a "pioneer preacher." When I was four years old he put my little sister and me in the back seat of a Model A Ford, and along with my mother struck out in response to his "call to preach." He took off not knowing where he was going, but was confident that God was leading him. We traveled around Oregon for several days until one day he drove over the crest of a little hill into a town where he felt "this was the place God had called him." He rented a lodge hall downtown that had a three-room apartment attached to the back. (Actually it was one room with three different colored linoleum floor coverings. The floor coverings denoted the rooms, so when my mother said, "You kids get out of the kitchen," we only had to go to the next colored linoleum and we were in the living room. The next linoleum took us into the bedroom. There was a closet off the bedroom where my father built beds on the wall for my sister and me to sleep.)

Every day my mother and father would go visiting, or as we said in those days, "calling", throughout the town inviting people to the new church. My sister and I would accompany them. We would have church every night. I often say that I have been in the ministry for over sixty years, but always qualify that by saying that I have been in the ministry since I was four years old. My father had the ability to include me in what he was doing. I thought that was the way to raise children, so I did the same when my son arrived on the scene.

My son and I had a great relationship while he was growing up. I included him in my visitation, especially in the rest homes. He always accompanied me to church on Sunday mornings as we went early. As he grew up he became the "temple boy", opening doors, turning on lights, preparing communion, etc. It was a good time for a father and son. I am happy today to see him involved in ministry as a pastor in a thriving, growing church, and also serving as an adjunct faculty member at Northwest College.

A life-changing experience occurred in my life at age four. My father had somehow secured a piece of property on which to build a new church. This transpired while we were still meeting in the small lodge hall downtown. After securing this property he accumulated one hundred dollars in the building fund. I have often said, "All you need to build a new church is one hundred dollars, and God. If you don't have God in your plans you can have a million dollars and fail, but 'with God all things are possible.'" My father took the one hundred dollars and dug out the ground for the basement and got the forms ready to pour the footings and foundation but had used all of the meager funds that had been accumulated in the building fund.

I remember one particular Sunday morning he stopped in

the service to "raise funds" for the purpose of buying cement now that the forms were prepared for the footings and basement walls. I can remember well that cement in those days cost one dollar a sack. I have no idea what cement costs today, but am certain of the price of that day. The reason I remember so well is that I had personally accumulated a "vast amount" of personal wealth ... I had one hundred pennies. Don't ask me, being raised at the end of the Great Depression and the son of a pioneer preacher, how I had accumulated this great amount of wealth, but I had. I know ... I counted them every day.

While sitting on the front row of the church that day, taking care of my little sister who was two years old, my mother was playing the piano and my father was conducting the service, God spoke to me. My father was soliciting responses to buy sacks of cement and people were responding. One person said they would buy five, another ten, and another man who was quite affluent for those days said he would buy twenty-five. That brought a considerable response of joy from the congregation. All of a sudden I sensed God speaking to my four-year-old heart, and He said, "You can buy one." I remembered my one hundred pennies and quite an internal struggle began. I now say that in my arguing with God I told Him, "That is my total life savings." He said, "I know." "But, God", I said, "That is my college education. That is what I am getting married with." I am sure that my reluctance was not measured in those terms.

Finally after some moments of struggle I lifted my hand. My father did not see my upraised hand for some time and finally recognized me, asking me what I wanted. I informed him I would buy one. I know that God loves a cheerful giver, but I went back to our living quarters after the service, counted my pennies for the final time, and cried all afternoon. That evening I brought my one hundred pennies and laid them on the altar and something happened in my young heart that night that never went away. From that day to this my life has been involved in one thing, the work of the Lord and His Church. I have endeavored to be a single-minded, single-purpose-individual.

Through my pastoral experience, years of traveling involved in churches, a variety of speaking opportunities, and being part of a church that was recognized for two consecutive years as the "fastest growing church in the state of Oregon" of all denominations, I am leaving some principles that I have learned, practiced and seen work. In no way do I claim to have all the answers, but have discovered some principles that have led to growth in the church.

I am extremely interested in the subject of Church Growth. I believe that Church Growth is a science. I believe that there are keys that, if we can find them, will work for me as they have worked for others. I am not talking about mind-trips and manipulation. I am talking about God-given principles and keys. You see, God has set in motion in this universe the laws of gravity, the laws of centrifugal force, and other natural laws.

These are laws that cannot be changed. People talk about individuals breaking God's laws. You can defy God's laws but you cannot break them. They will break you, but you will not break them because those laws are unchangeable. They will always remain the same. I don't care how spiritual you feel, you will never get up on a high building and say, "Folks I have never been so close to God, I am going to fly off this building" and take a big leap and fly. You will splatter on the ground below because of the undeniable law of gravity that is in operation.

I don't care how well designed your car is, there is a certain limit on a corner when you will break through the wall of centrifugal force and your car will go over the bank no matter how well that car is designed and engineered. Your car may go a little faster than mine, but there is a limit designed into that car that is bound by the law of centrifugal force. You are not going to break the law. You are going to break your neck, probably, but not the law of centrifugal force. Those are universal laws. There are moral laws that God has written in this universe. You will not break the moral laws of God. People are defying those laws today, and they are the ones who are being broken ... broken physically, broken emotionally, broken spiritually, and even broken financially because they are defying the unbreakable laws of God.

I believe also, within the church, there are laws that have been established. My wife knows my interest in the subject of Church Growth and is continually buying me books for special days. I have a growing section in my library on the subject. I am reading about it all the time. I am studying successful people and successful churches. I think we ought to find winners and find out what winners are doing. Don't look at a bunch of losers and say, "I think I am better than he is." Hitch your wagon to a star and try to find the best. Find somebody to model who has achieved and excelled in greater ways than you. That is what I have endeavored to do in life.

I am a person who asks a lot of questions. Whenever I am with successful people I ask them questions. As a young pastor I had a very successful pastor come to conduct a series of meetings in our church. I must have bored him with all of my questions. I asked him why he did not set pre-service seminars for different groups in the church. He replied, "You are the first person who has asked me any questions. Everyone seems to give the impression that they have it all figured out and have all the answers." What a tragedy. There were several life-changing things that happened to me during those days when I had the privilege to be with that successful pastor.

Now, I have told you about the Church Growth section in my library. I could develop a bibliography for you on the subject, but you can do that easily through any bookstore. Though I have read a lot of books on church growth, the best book I have ever read on the subject is the Book of Acts in the New Testament of the Bible. I invite you to look with me into that Book as we examine these "Twenty-One Positive Principles for a Powerful Twenty-First Century Church." Each chapter will begin with a Scripture reference from the Book of Acts to serve as a foundation for each of these "positive principles."

I had a godly, elderly professor in college who taught on the subject of Pneumatology (the study of the Holy Spirit). One day at the end of class he said, "I don't have an assignment for you before the next class. I just want you to go home and 'wallow around' in the book of Acts." I've never forgotten that. It's not a bad place to "wallow around." What he was trying to say is just let the Word of God get in you and over you, "wallow around" in it. I want to do that with you as we look together for these important principles that will guide us as we move through this exciting twenty-first century.

Let me share with you how this book was born. Several years ago I was on my way to assist a church while serving as District Superintendent. I took my father with me and reminded him of a sermon I had heard him preach when I was just a boy. We begin to review that sermon on this subject. When I arrived at the church I sat down on the front pew and jotted down seven "P's for a Powerful Church." Later I was asked to speak for a joint meeting with several churches and the message had grown to "Nine P's". It continued to grow. While I was speaking at a camp meeting I used the material and was up to sixteen principles by then. I said, "we really shouldn't quit at sixteen, we should have twenty-one as we move into a new century." Those folks in that morning teaching session helped me as I added the final five to round out the full twenty-one. So all of these principles will begin with the letter "P" as we develop these principles.

We are going through incredible changes as we have entered the "Information Age." However, there are some principles that remain timeless.

I have always wanted to be a change agent, but not merely for the sake of change. We will discuss some of the pain of change in a later chapter.

If, after reading this book, I can be of personal counsel to you, I would be happy to assist you in anyway I can. My desire is to spend the remaining years of my life in assisting churches and pastors and would be honored to consult with you.

Chapter One

A PENITENT CHURCH

"Peter replied, 'Repent and be baptized, everyone one of you, in the name of Jesus Christ so that your sins may be forgiven. And you will receive the gift of the Holy Spirit'" (Acts 2:38).

The foundation of the New Testament church is laid upon the premise that we begin with a fellowship of people who have had a personal encounter with the Living Lord Jesus. The heart of the message of Pentecost was that Jesus Christ had come to be the only Savior and that the entrance into this Fellowship was through the atoning sacrifice He made at Calvary and the fact that He had risen from the dead.

The first quality for a powerful 21st century church is that they were a penitent church. It is impossible to have a strong church without leadership that has been born-again by the Spirit of God. A church that is going to advance and meet the needs of a desperately hurting world will only be successful as they are led by spiritual people. Our challenge today is a spiritual challenge. "For our struggle is not against flesh and blood, but against the rulers, against the authorities, against the powers of this dark world and against the spiritual forces of evil in the heavenly realms" (Ephesians 6:12).

Please don't misunderstand me. I feel that there is a vast difference between the church (the called out ones) and those in attendance at what we commonly call a "church meeting." Our public meetings are more than the "church" coming together. It is the result of the church that has been in action and touching the lives of their non-churched family, friends, neighbors, business associates, etc. Ideally when we come together for our public meetings there should be an equal number of unbelievers as there are believers in attendance. This will become a reality if we are having the influence we should in the world. Each one of us should have influenced at least one person during the week who would be with us the following Sunday.

I will talk about this in later chapters, but if spiritual leadership would give opportunity in every service for people to respond by personally receiving Christ there would undoubtedly be more people present who needed Christ. When the membership of the church realizes the importance leadership is placing on conversion it will be a motivator in bringing their friends and acquaintances with them. The procedure of bringing people to a place of decision and their response is not nearly as important as just doing it. I have a personal approach that seemed to fit my personality and brought spiritual results, but I have read other interesting approaches that have similar, if not greater results.

In my desire to make this book practical in nature allow me to share my particular approach to the end of the sermon. I have often said I built my sermons from the end to the beginning. After reviewing the text/passage from where I was preaching, I would ascertain how the message could conclude with an invitation for a response from those who needed Christ as their Savior. I would ask for a showing of hands of those who wanted/needed to receive Christ into their lives. We would ask the entire congregation to pray a "sinner's prayer." Often I would ask that heads would remain bowed and ask again to those who had previously responded, and any others who had in sincerity prayed the prayer, to raise their hands again indicating that this was their personal prayer. I would then explain to them what had transpired in their lives and conclude by expressing the need to publicly confess Christ as their Savior. I would state that the way we have chosen to do that today is to merely come and stand facing the front. I assured them that they would not be asked to say anything, but that by coming and standing they were saying that they were now a Christian. We had over one hundred people trained to respond with them. I would always assure them that they were not coming alone and that others would be coming with them. The closing song would be introduced with the encouragement to step out on the first word. Suddenly the aisles would be filled with our trained people, known as the "Friendship Force", which created a positive move toward the front. The "Friendship Force" did not identify themselves in anyway that they were anyone other than one of those coming to confess Christ.

I would have a personal word to share with all at the altar followed by a closing benediction either by a pastor or the choir. During this time I would leave to be at the door to greet the congregation as they were leaving. I would always state just before the benediction that there were those standing close to them who had some helpful materials to leave with them and to please remain for a moment. At the conclusion of the benediction our people (the Friendship Force) would engage those who had come forward in dialogue, giving them material and securing information from them so that they could be followed up with after their decision.

I would encourage you to read Rick Warren's book, "The

Purpose Driven Church" to see the approach that is so successfully used at Saddleback Community Church. I believe that the invitation time must suit your personal style and community. Whatever we do there is no spirituality in making that moment embarrassing or more difficult than it needs to be. There is a spiritual battle going on in the hearts of people when they are making such a drastic move in their lives. We must be part of the redeeming, caring heart of Jesus in that moment rather than joining the side of that which would keep them from making a proper response.

So, the church is not just for the redeemed but the leadership of the church must be. This is abundantly clear in the formation of the New Testament church. There was no expressed desire to select individuals to positions of leadership who had "connections" or were politically correct. Every decision for leadership positions was carefully prayed about and the affirmation of the Holy Spirit was seriously sought. This was no popularity contest.

There are churches that are growing and having powerful impacts in local communities who are being accused by much less significant groups as being "soft on sin" and that is the reason for their growth. The accusation states that they have no standards so that is why people come, as there is no demand for commitment, it is said. What I have discovered in my experience, both as a long-term pastor of a major church and a denominational leader, is that the larger church is often much more selective in their leadership than the smaller church. One of the obvious reasons is that there is a larger pool of potential people to serve. I saw some deplorable things as a district superintendent. I discovered people in places of leadership who were totally unfit.

May I leave a word of advice for ministers who find themselves pastoring in close proximity to a larger mega-church? If you will treat that church and minister with respect, they will bless you. Let's face it, not everyone is going to identify with the larger church. While that church has been the attraction that may have introduced a person to Christ, after a period of time there is a certain type of individual that will choose to go be part of a smaller congregation where it would appear they would have more intimacy.

Treat the pastor of that larger church with respect. Speak in positive ways about that ministry. When you speak about the church or pastor in a negative way you will have people attend there and find they have been misinformed. The law of harvest will always remain true ... "whatsoever you sow that will you also reap."

Spiritual leadership will produce spiritual leadership. By this I mean that when the tone of the church is established, people will seek to maintain a level of spirituality that God is honoring. There is always a concern during the nominating process, but I found that people involved in the selective procedure were very sensitive that spiritual people be in places of leadership. That is one of the secrets of a powerful church.

I always informed the nominating committee that the pastor had "veto power" if he needed it. I never did. However, there are times that a pastor has confidential information that might disqualify certain individuals from places of responsibility. I remember times when I said to the committee, "I think perhaps we should wait upon our thinking of this person", or "Perhaps next year would be a better time to make this consideration."

After the nominations were completed and before they were presented to a congregational meeting I, as pastor, always interviewed the nominees. I would ask three succinct questions: First, would you serve if elected? (What a stroke of brilliance to ask such a question. Seriously, why would a person be selected who was not willing to serve?) I had some interesting responses through the years to that question. One man said he would rather not be considered because he was afraid it would affect his ministry. When I inquired about his ministry he said, "Oh, pastor, you know I teach the three-year-olds and that is the most important thing I know. I'm afraid that by serving on the board of deacons it would rob me of time I should give to those children." Another man when asked replied, "I've had the honor to do that before and it is a great privilege to work so close to you, but I think we should give some younger men that same privilege." With that kind of spirit it is no wonder that God could bless a church.

My next question, "Do you agree with the philosophy of ministry and leadership that God has placed in this church?" I would add to my question that if they were not in harmony with the direction the church was going it would be a waste of their time and mine if they were in a place of leadership. I was not looking for "yes" individuals, but people who had an understanding and commitment to the direction and philosophy of the church.

My final question, "Are you a tither?" I believe that no one should be in a place of leadership who is not supporting the church. Perhaps this information should have been gleaned during the nominating process, but it was often postponed to the time of the pastoral interview.

In summary, it would appear that the importance of spiritual leadership is clearly validated by the bottom-line of Peter's message at Pentecost. That event we look back to as the birth of the church, began with the message of repentance to insure that the church was begun with a people who had been regenerated by the power of God.

Chapter Two

A PERSERVERING CHURCH

"They continued steadfast in the apostles' doctrine and fellowship, and in breaking of bread, and in prayers" (Acts 2:42 KJV).

They persevered.
Leadership today is being challenged by the apparent lack of dedication and loyalty in the lives of people. Our transitory society, our affluence and time for a myriad of recreational pursuits, has depleted the core of faithful, dependable people in the local church. This is not just a problem within the church, but is a problem in our society in general. I am a long-standing member of a service club and I am seeing the difficulty of attracting younger business people to make a commitment for this kind of association.

I am not discouraged with this apparent lack of dependability and commitment. I am witnessing on the part of a great number of young people a strong desire to give of themselves in service through the local church.

I love what we read here in the Book of Acts. These people who were instrumental in building this powerful church continued to meet together in the temple courts. These people stuck with it. They continued. They were persevering.

Let me leave you a law of life. Life is not all "ups", there are down times in life too. It is not only a law of life, but it is a law in the church. It's a law in your business. It certainly is a law in your marriage. But you see, everybody wants everything to always be on the up, up, up. Lucy, the cartoon character in the comic strips, Peanuts, said, to Charlie Brown one day, "Life has its ups and downs." Charlie Brown replied, "I know that but I don't want downs. I just want ups, ups, and more ups." Don't we all!

There is a great little verse in the Old Testament that fascinates me and illustrates my point. When the children of Israel were on their way out of Egypt, the Lord said to them, "The land you are ... to take possession of is a land of mountains and valleys ..." (Deuteronomy 11:11) That's life. Ups and downs. Humps and slumps. And the sooner we learn that lesson the better off we are going to be. That's what happens in marriages today. There are a lot of crucial moments in the marriage relationship. Some of those who work in that arena to strengthen marriages talk of the seventh year of a marriage as a critical period. Hence the term, "the seven year itch."

Through the years I have had people come to my office and announce, "We're getting a divorce." I respond, "Oh really? What's the problem?" "Well, we just don't love each other any more." And I ask, "What else is new? Since when is your relationship to marriage based on love? I thought you had made a commitment." The problem was they were basing their love on a feeling. They were not on this "upper" any more and now they are on some kind of a downer and they think it is time to break up a relationship. My marriage is not built on how I feel, but is built on a commitment I made over 40 years ago.

I believe that same kind of commitment needs to be made

in our relationship with the church. Not only to the church universal, but to the local church.

We must realize that in the church it is not always going to be on an "upper".

I started pastoring a church the day after I left college. I wasn't married yet. I had announced my engagement to be married and with that in mind I think the church signed me up to be their pastor knowing that I had a wife waiting in the wings. I assumed the pastorate of this little church and will not go into how I finished my tenure there except to report an incident that occurred on the morning that I announced my resignation. A young deacon came to me following the service and announced, "I'm resigning, too. I'm leaving. I only stayed because of you." I said, "You can't do that." He responded, "But I am tired. I have worked so hard in this church that now I am going to go too." I encouraged him, "You know, this church really needs you. You can't do that. You've got to remain faithful."

That young man was giving twenty five percent of his income to the church. He was driving 70 miles every Sunday bringing his family and picking up other people. He had never missed a single service the entire time I was there. He never missed an extended service, a youth rally, or a united meeting of our Fellowship. He worked six days a week in a mill and still exhibited that kind of faithfulness. (I'll tell you about their faithfulness, which I certainly didn't demand. His wife played the piano on Wednesday evening for the service, had a baby on Thursday, and was back playing the piano on Sunday.) I only said to him, "You can't leave."

Years later, Nancy, my wife, and I were invited back for the 50th anniversary of that church. The night we were there this man was present with his wife and ten children. They continued to have babies after we left. Obviously we didn't discourage that when we left! All ten of those children, some were now grown and away from home and in ministry, others involved in serving God in other capacities, and all Christians, were there. They had a little choir and sang. If you have ten children you can have a choir! With a family that size you can have a lot of things ... you can have two basketball teams, you can have a baseball team, and if dad gets out there you can have a whole football team. Large families are tremendous in what they can do. Here was this family, all together, all loving the church, and all serving God. That's the reward of persistence.

Later we were invited back again. The congregation had built a lovely new church building. The church had tripled in attendance under new and dynamic leadership. I was asked to preach the dedicatory sermon celebrating the completion of this new facility. Coming down the aisle with the other ushers was this same man. He had stuck with it. Believe me, it was not always exciting in that little church. I have a feeling there were times when his children were the total youth group in the church. But, it paid off. Here was an entire family serving God.

While serving as president of Northwest College I had a vice-president serving with me who joined the administrative team during my tenure. I did not know him before he came to assume his duties. However, I had the wonderful privilege to be his parents' pastor for twenty years. I had performed the wedding ceremonies for some of his siblings, conducted the funeral services for his grandparents, and had only seen him at these occasions. His father is one of the greatest men of integrity I have ever met. I don't know a finer man. He had suffered a business failure years before I ever knew him. He raised his family very frugally. They never went on any exotic vacations, never did any extravagant things. This man probably should have declared bankruptcy and then gone back and done what he did. However, after his business failure he systematically paid off all of his creditors, and it took him years. I would imagine it took at least 20 years to pay them off. I am convinced that if he would have claimed bankruptcy he would have done the same thing.

By the way, I personally believe that is the Christian position to take. I remember the day when this man came to me and said, "It's all over. I just paid off the last debt." You see, this kind of persistence modeled before children has a positive effect on their faith and behavior.

When my son was quite small, and I hadn't been in Salem very long, I had been very quiet about raising kids. Nancy and I were married five years when our son was born. Before his birth I was quite an authority on raising children. Then we had one and I went into about a 21 year hiatus and nobody heard much personal counsel about raising children because I wanted to see how this one would turn out. I have jokingly said, "Now I am back in the business again telling everyone how to do it." Seriously, our project turned out quite well and my confidence level is back.

Let me continue. The night I was teaching and talking on this subject of raising children, this man and his wife were sitting in front of me. I stopped and asked, "Could you folks please tell us how you raised such a nice family?" He responded, "You know, my wife and I were talking about that the other day and we can't figure it out." He went on to say, "We came to the conclusion that there is only one thing that we can identify. Every time the doors of this church are open we are all here as a family." That's the only thing he could identify ... persistence and faithfulness.

As an observer of this family I could have identified additional things. But I have to tell you, it wasn't always exciting to be there. The church wasn't always exciting. But those children had the wonderful privilege of watching a man of integrity, watching a mother and father who put God first in everything. Today all of those children are Christians. They are all involved in the life of the church. You tell me how much that is worth. To me that is worth everything. I would rather have that as an outcome of sacrifice and steadfastness than anything I know of in this world. There is nothing more rewarding than to witness seeing our families serving God.

I was sharing some of these thoughts in a church and met a man who reminded me that we had met several years previous in that same church. He had received Christ as his personal Savior on Easter Sunday, and I had come to speak the following week. He reminded me that I told him, in response to his question on how he could grow spiritually, (I think I told him while addressing the entire congregation) "If you want to grow and if you want to develop in your relationship with God, then you occupy that seat and you be there every time the doors are open. I promise you that you will grow." He came up to me and said, "I remember what you told me and I did it." Now some years later I met him in this same setting and observed a mature, yet continuing to grow and develop Christian. That is the way growth comes in our lives and it is the way growth is manifested throughout the whole church, when we who are the core and part of that living, vital church, are steadfast. Then God will bless us as He blesses others.

I love that inspirational poem from the unknown author ...

DON'T QUIT!

When things go wrong, as they sometimes will,
When the road you're trudging seems all uphill,
When the funds are low and the debts are high,
And you want to smile, but you have to sigh,
When care is pressing you down a bit
Rest if you must, but don't you quit.
Life is strange with its twists and turns,
As every one of us sometimes learns,

And many a person turns about
When he might have won had he stuck it out.
Don't give up though the pace seems slow—
You may succeed with another blow.

Often the goal is nearer than
It seems to a faint and faltering man;
Often the struggler has given up
When he might have captured the victor's cup;
And he learned too late when the night came down
How close he was to the golden crown.

And we've all been tempted.

I know what it means to be discouraged. I know what it means to dream dreams and have them not come to pass or be delayed for a long time. I know what it means to have people turn their back on you. I know when other people's doubts can almost cause you to begin to doubt yourself and your God-given dreams.

Shortly after I went to Salem, Oregon to pastor, I made the discovery that the present church facilities would never be adequate to get the job done that needed to be accomplished in that city. However, I had a problem. The congregation had recently moved into a new church facility after a large commitment of sacrifice and determination. Prior to my coming they had moved into this new facility. Shortly after moving in their pastor, who had led them in this tremendous project and step of faith, was killed in a private plane crash, along with two other prominent men of the congregation. It was a tremendous blow to that church to lose their dynamic pastor/leader. After moving into their new building in September this tragedy occurred in December. The building, though occupied, had large areas to finish. One entire floor was boarded up and no permit had been issued for that area to be occupied.

An associate pastor of the church was elected to serve as the pastor and remained for over two years in what in reality was an interim situation. Upon my arrival to begin pastoral duties I discovered that there had been no work done to complete the building since the death of the previous pastor. We proceeded to finish the building and acquired additional property surrounding the church. We became aware that there was only one hope for any consistent growth and that was to relocate. That was a frightening thought. Here we were in a new building and how would the congregation ever consider another move?

While away from the city at a conference, The Robert Schuller Institute For Successful Church Leadership, at three o'clock in the morning, I believe I heard from God. Please understand, I have never heard the audible voice of God. I've only had four or five times in my life when I think God definitely spoke to me and that was deep in my spirit. But, in this early morning hour I really felt that God was talking to me. I was excited. I couldn't sleep. I got up from my bed and wrote down a plan how to present the options for the future of the church. I came home, called for a special business meeting of the church, and we discussed our future and what we could do to reach our city.

I gave them four options that night, only one being to relocate. I had two overhead projectors operating. I had the four options presented, one at a time on one projector and the estimated cost on the other, until I got to the final option which was to relocate. Next to that option, instead of a dollar amount, I just put, "total commitment." I knew it was going to cost millions of dollars. We began to discuss all of these options and had a very open forum that night in the business meeting. The outcome of the meeting proved to be the most emotional night of my life.

A man, for whom I had prayed and asked God to never allow him to serve on the church board, got up in that meeting. (I since have told him of my feelings. Looking back, I had totally misread him. I thought he was a negative person.) He stood to his feet and proceeded to say, "When we moved into this church building we had to mortgage our houses, we drove old cars, we had to sit on broken down furniture, and we couldn't even buy a new suit of clothes. We gave everything to this project and I think it would be a dirty shame now ..." I stood there and breathed a silent prayer, "Oh God, shut him up!" He continued, "...now we should let the next generation do the same thing." Just as an aside, that man probably invested more in that relocation project than any other person in that church. He certainly put his money where his mouth was.

There were several more meaningful comments made by some of the original members of the church. I will be forever grateful to those marvelous people who exercised such faith. The vote was taken. All four of the propositions were voted on simultaneously. They all received some votes, but the vote to relocate received 93 percent of all votes cast. We were on our way. I wish I could tell you that we broke ground the next day, but that is not how it happened. I went through about six years of real testing.

In a chapter I wrote, *Obstacles in the Life of the Pastor*, as a contributor to the book, THE PENTECOSTAL PASTOR (Gospel Publishing House, Springfield, Missouri, 1997), I shared some of the waiting time we went through. I share those days with you here:

In my eighth year, of my twenty year tenure as pastor of The People's Church in Salem, Oregon, I went through one of the darkest times of my life. The congregation had voted with a strong majority to relocate. We were in a nearly new building at that time close to the downtown core. It was determined that if we were to impact our city we needed to relocate as we had very limited off-street parking. The faith of the congregation was expressed in their vote to move forward after a time of great sacrifice to get where they were. The vote was taken ... the new acreage on the edge of the city was purchased ... architectural drawings were completed ...pictures of the finished facility were displayed ... and nothing happened. I felt it was imperative that we sell our present facility before we became involved in a multimillion dollar expansion and relocation.

Months went by. In the middle of this time a church called me, as they were looking for a pastor. They presented an exciting opportunity. I told them later that if I ever wrote a book on "How to Get a Pastor" that I would give them an entire chapter. They were impressive in all they did ... sending their daily city newspaper to my home for a month ... a different person calling me every day for a week ... putting my wife and me in a penthouse on the top floor of a hotel during a visit.

During this decision time Dr. Robert Schuller came to our city to speak. The sponsoring group asked me if I would introduce him as I had had some contact with him through his Institute for Successful Church Leadership. He arrived just in time to speak and we had very little time to visit. On the way to the stage I told him my dilemma how I could not get this project off the ground and the wonderful opportunity that had been presented to me to move.

He asked, "How long have you been here?"

I replied, "Eight years."

He said, "Do you mean you are going to throw away an eight-year investment and start over again?"

I had told him that the Chamber of Commerce of the other city had informed me that their city was going to quadruple in ten years. He said, "If that town quadruples, this town will double in the same period of time."

He then reached in his pocket, pulled out a coin and thrust it into my hand and said, "Take this and build that church for God. If you don't, nobody else will." By then we were walking on the stage.

After the meeting I pulled the coin out of my pocket and read three verses of Scripture on one side ...

"Be still, and know that I am God" (Ps. 46:10).[1]

"If God is for us, who can be against us?" (Rom. 8:31).

"I will not die but live ..." (Ps. 118:17)

On the other side was this prayer:

"Thank you, God ... for solving so many of my problems in the past. Please God, help me today. I need you and I trust you. Amen."[2]

That evening was a turning point for me. Dr. Schuller became God's voice to me to remain faithful to the place where He had placed me.

A few days later I went home in the evening and found an unlighted house. I looked through the house and found Nancy, my wife, in the back bathroom, crying. I asked her, "What is the matter?" She answered, "You have a wonderful opportunity to get out of here, and I say 'let's go.'" I replied, "Nancy, I can't. If I leave now I will spend the rest of my life wondering what would have happened if I had stayed. I am going to stay and prove that it can't be done if that is the case." Through her tears she said, "I knew you would say that. I don't think you're committed, I think you're stubborn." We have laughed many times about that night and our hour of deep discouragement.

I will not go into the details of how God solved our problem. Not ours only, but He took care of some big problems for several other groups in our city at the same time as we sold our downtown property and made the move.

On the day we moved into that multi-million dollar facility, I spoke on the subject, "THE COIN THAT BUILT A TWO MILLION DOLLAR CHURCH!", referring to that divine encounter I had with Robert Schuller.

I am convinced that we will never see our dreams come true without persevering. We can make excuses and blame others, but persevering pays off. We can blame others while we may have failed because we lacked patience. I saw a cartoon in an airline magazine and the hare (rabbit) was seated at a bar and the bartender said to him, "They have discovered the real reason is that the turtle was on steroids." We know what the real reason was ... the hare quit before the finish line and the persevering of the tortoise paid off with the victory.

Chapter Three

A PARTNERING CHURCH

Acts 2:42 *"THEY devoted THEMSELVES to the apostles' teaching and to the fellowship ..."*

verse 44 *"ALL the believers were TOGETHER and had everything in common."*

There is a biblical principle that starts way back at the place of beginnings. After God created the first man, He said, "It is not good for man to be alone." God never expected any of us to be alone in our work. He has not called us to be involved in His work without the assistance, strength, camaraderie, and support we receive from someone else.

Look through the Bible and see the long list of those who partnered together ... Adam and Eve, Moses and Aaron, Caleb and Joshua, David and Jonathan, Ruth and Naomi, Esther and Mordecai, Daniel and his three Hebrew friends, Paul and Silas, Barnabas and Mark.

Jesus set the example by surrounding Himself with His friends, whom we call disciples. When he was introducing them to their personal involvement in ministry He sent them out "two by two." We gain strength from unity and cooperation.

Beware of the person who avoids contact with their peers. Beware of the minister who becomes so busy and occupied with the "ministry" that he no longer has time to become involved in fellowship with other members of the clergy. I learned a great lesson that impacted my life and ministry through the late Tony Fontaine. At that time Tony was on the concert tour, had recently completed the film, "The Tony Fontaine Story" and was serving as vice-president of the Screen Actors Guild in Hollywood. He had come to our church to conduct a five-day crusade. The Baptist churches in our city were planning a united evangelistic meeting in the city's largest auditorium. After all the plans were made, the meeting scheduled and things in motion for the beginning of the crusade, an invitation was extended for all the other churches to join them. Honestly, I had some hesitancy. My reluctance was born out of my own negative thinking that said, "If they really wanted us to be a part of this crusade, why didn't they ask us in the first place."

I sought the counsel of Tony Fontaine and asked him what I should do with the invitation. His reply changed my life and thinking in the future. He said, "Anytime anyone is trying to reach people for Christ, help them." I did. I joined in the crusade effort. The sponsoring group asked if the crusade evangelist could preach in our pulpit on Sunday morning during the crusade. It was a great time in our city. Many churches benefited, but none benefited more than ours. God used that crusade in our city to bring unity among us.

Partnership creates accountability. We need someone to hold us accountable. Many of us have lived through a period when we witnessed some great failures in the lives of prominent people. Closer partnering could have, and undoubtedly would have, prevented some of these tragedies and embarrassments to the work of God.

Please don't allow me to put myself up as some marvelous example, but I have had the wonderful joy of being involved through my years of ministry with a great number of very dedicated people. For thirteen years I never missed a Tuesday morning gathering with a group of men in the back room of a little downtown restaurant. Those men became closer to me than any brother. After being gone from Salem for over ten years, I was back in the city to attend a luncheon and early that morning I dropped into the back room of that little restaurant and found several of those same men, along with new faces to me. What a joy it was to join those prayer partners again.

For twenty years as the senior pastor in a church I had the privilege to work closely with those who were chosen to serve on the Board of Deacons. In twenty years we never had one dissenting vote in a board meeting. Someone asked me, "How do you see something like that occur?" My answer is very simple. Don't vote on everything! When you are in partnership you have the freedom to seek the counsel of those around you, to listen in open and honest dialogue, and then to come to the place of good and godly decisions. As a leader one needs to know when to "table" an idea. This can be done without formal resolution, but by the leader just moving to the next item on the agenda. There are not many things worth dying for. There are not many things worth dividing a group of people over. It was interesting that some of those "tabled" items were brought back three or six months later, often by someone who had expressed the greatest degree of reluctance. Some items never came back, because they were not of life and death importance in the first place.

Satan can destroy, tempt, or discourage us when we are alone. We gain strength through partnerships. It is interesting that Jesus spent the last night of His life before His trial and death with His friends, the disciples. He ate with them.

He told them the deep anguish of His heart. How do we know the anguish He felt in the Garden? We know because He came out of that experience and shared it with them. He must have said, "Guys do you know what it is like to carry the sins of the world upon you? Do you know what it means to feel the loneliness of being removed from God's presence?" They certainly weren't alert enough to sense the depths of what was occurring without Him sharing with them the impact of that moment. His sharing must have made some kind of impact as we see the account recorded by these men who became the gospel writers. We would have never known the anguish that Jesus experienced if he had not shared it with His friends.

Many times when we are going through a sorrow, or have been tempted and failed, or have used poor judgment in a situation, Satan comes to accuse us and endeavors to separate us from the place of fellowship. It is at those times that we need the strength that comes from others. Fear and failure lock us up behind closed doors and robs us of the presence of the Living Christ even as the disciples were shut away immediately following the resurrection.

Chapter Four

A PRAYING CHURCH

I n Acts 4:31 we read, *"And after they prayed, the place where they were meeting was shaken and they were all filled with the Holy Spirit and spoke the word of God boldly."*

Prayer was the bottom line of Pentecost. The people had been praying for ten days as they waited in the Upper Room. Every "Pentecost" is birthed in the prayer meeting.

There are wonderful reports of revival coming from all over the world. Thankfully this includes the United States of America as well. Without exception, every report of revival is accompanied by the fact that the people had been praying. Sometimes those prayer meetings had been going on for months. One of the early signs of revival is an increase in the number of people who begin attending the prayer meetings.

Often in our desire to see the moving of God's Spirit among us we get discouraged that so few people seem interested in the prayer meeting. We must remember that preceding the New Testament revival that birthed the church there were only 120 who were praying. On the first day of that revival 3,000 responded to receive Jesus through repentance. God has never worked through the masses, but has always found faithful people who were willing to pray.

We have all been intrigued by the growth of the world's largest church in Seoul, Korea, The Full Gospel Church, pastored by Paul Yongii Cho. The numbers continue to grow and it is difficult to put the number on record, but their membership is somewhere around 800,000. If you have had the privilege to visit that church, as I have, hopefully you took a side trip to Prayer Mountain where they have around the clock praying and services. When you walk among the little "caves" in the mountain designed for personal prayer you hear the mountain hum with the sound of prayer being offered. I'm sure that if you asked Dr. Cho today the secret of the fantastic growth in that church he would say, "Prayer."

While serving as president of Northwest College I had the privilege of taking eleven young ministerial students to the Robert H. Schuller Institute For Successful Church Leadership in Garden Grove, California. Dr. Schuller was kind enough to give these young students a personal visit in his office that was scheduled before they went to the Institute. He asked them what questions they would like to ask him. One of them, looking out of his office window of the 12th floor of the Tower of Hope overlooking the campus, asked, "How did all of this happen." Dr. Schuller immediately answered with one word, "Prayer." Then he added, "Goals will guide your life, but if your goals are set in prayer then God will control your life."

When asked further about his prayer life he responded, "God and I talk with each other all during the day. He speaks to me and guides me in my decisions and dreams." (I would encourage you to read Dr. Schuller's book, "Prayer ... My Soul's Adventure with God." In that book he talks about the "Seven Levels of Prayer.")

During my time as president of Northwest College as my schedule would permit, I would periodically go to Life Center in Tacoma, Washington to speak or to attend the services, where Dr. Fulton Buntain has pastored for over 30 years. There has never been a time when attending there that I have not been impacted with the presence of God. Again, early in the year I attended and heard Pastor Buntain making an appeal again for people to join the "Thousand Band." This is a group of people who commit to pray daily for the church. He was making the appeal and reporting that over 1,200 had responded, but he was encouraging others to join. Is it any wonder that there is an awareness of God's presence in the place?

I'm fascinated with the reports of revivals that are occurring in our day. I must concur with what someone said regarding the trips that are being made to particular places to witness this visitation from God, that rather than making trips perhaps we need to do what preceded these manifestations with protracted periods of prayer. It appears that we believe somehow that a revival can occur by following some procedure when every true revival has been preceded by prayer. Prayer has always been the prerequisite of revival. Let's pray!!!

In a following chapter we will talk about the principle of "preaching." I am convinced that there will be no spiritual results from any presentation/preaching of God's Word that is not accompanied by, and preceded with, prayer. There must be an accompanying anointing to the preaching of the Word, and that anointing always comes through prayer.

At the conclusion of a service where I was speaking as a guest we gave the invitation where a good number of people responded as we sang, "Just As I Am." Someone came up to me at the close of the service and said, "We haven't heard that song sung for many years."

I shared that comment with my secretary and she made an interesting statement. "There is a special anointing in that song." I had never thought about it before. I have sung that song hundreds and hundreds of times in my ministry. Billy

Graham uses that song every night at the close of his crusade service. Then I got to thinking, "Maybe she's got something. Maybe there is an anointing that is carried in that song because thousands and thousands of people have responded to Christ at the singing of that simple invitation song." But, it takes more than a song being sung, it takes an anointing and drawing of the Holy Spirit that is a response to prayer.

It is thrilling to witness that magnetic atmosphere in a church service. That is not hype ... it is the Holy Spirit. People praying is what makes it all happen. That is why people come to a church. When they are invited there is a response from them ignited by the Holy Spirit to accept the invitation. When the Spirit has drawn them, then when the pastor stands up and speaks, somehow it all connects and relates. That is God. That is the Holy Spirit. That is not the talent of a man. It is the Spirit of God that is at work in people's lives. And it all happens because somebody is praying. That New Testament church was a praying, powerful church that produced those kinds of spiritual results.

What we are witnessing in our world today we would not have dreamed about a few years ago as it relates to revival. When I was a young man we were all afraid of a communist takeover. These fears were fueled by Nikita Khrushchev, the dynamic Russian leader. He came to this country and at the United Nations, took his shoe off and pounded the table and said, "We will bury you!" And all of us just shook in our boots. We knew it was coming, we just didn't know when. We knew the horrible communists were about to bury us.

I believe the Almighty, Sovereign God took care of the problem. I will never believe that it was political maneuvering that brought down the Iron Curtain and the Berlin Wall. I believe it was God. I believe it was a response from the God of the universe to the prayers of people on planet Earth. Who knows how many Christians were praying. A quiet, rather insignificant man in the church where I was pastoring at the time, had a picture of Mikhail Gorbachev in his place of prayer where every day Gorbachev and the Russians were prayed for. That scene was replicated around the world.

I share in the social, moral, and political concerns we have as Christians. On the other hand I am totally convinced that our problems will not be solved by the politicians. They will not be solved by Christians joining marches. Legislation is not the answer. A change in political leadership is not the answer. The answer is found in changed lives and those who have been touched by the Living God.

If I were to develop a pastoral staff in the future, I would be tempted to place high priority on a person who is called the "Director of Prayer Ministries." If prayer is as important as we claim it to be, then perhaps it is time to find that gifted person to lead the way.

C. Peter Wagner writes about people in his book, *Your Spiritual Gifts Can Help Your Church Grow*, who are particularly gifted in prayer. Dr. Wagner lists twenty-seven different gifts. Interesting, he lists as number twenty-six the "Gift of Intercession."

When reading his account that Asbury Seminary has a Professor of Prayer and has students who are majoring in prayer, and Campus Crusade for Christ has eight full-time staff members in their Prayer-Care ministry who go to work at the prayer chapel at their headquarters and pray for eight hours and call it another day's work, I thought, "Why not?" We recognize other gifted individuals and create staff positions for people gifted in business administration, working with children and youth, music, and the list goes on and on. Why not create staff positions for people who are gifted in prayer? Allow them the freedom of not being burdened down with other duties to support a family and activities that do not use their gifts to the highest effectiveness.[3]

I do not share that idea as an excuse for the rest of us to relegate all of our praying to others. We all need to develop our prayer times. There is probably nothing that convicts me more than my prayerlessness. Yet I read that we are encouraged to "pray without ceasing." That is an impossible request, unless we develop some habits of prayer.

I have taught people the idea of "association prayer." Find those things that are common to our every day experience and use them as "triggers" to prayer. For instance, in the home whenever the refrigerator is touched that is a signal to pray. Whenever a traveling salesperson touches the turn signal, let it be used as a prompter to pray. I encouraged young people that while in school whenever they heard a bell ring that meant it was time to pray. When the bell rang to begin a class to lift a short prayer, saying, "Lord, live through me in this class. Keep my mind on you and not to be influenced by teaching that would rob me of my faith." When the class ended they were encouraged to lift a prayer when the bell rang, "Thank you Lord for being with me in this class. Bless me as I associate with my friends on the way to my next class. Let someone see Jesus in me."

A young man wrote to me who had graduated from the United States Coast Guard Academy in Kings Point, New York. He told me after his graduation, "If you had not taught me how to pray with my eyes open and to pray on my feet, I would have never made it. For four years I have never been alone. There has been somebody with me every second of my life. But you taught me how to pray with my eyes open. You taught me how to pray in a crowd. You taught me how to recognize the presence of God with me, that Jesus was right there in my bunk, walking with me, marching with me, out in the ship with me. He was with me. I had learned how to communicate with Him and to know He was there." That young man practiced the presence of God. And that's prayer.

Prayer is not a position of the body. Prayer is a condition of the soul and a relationship we develop as we communicate with God.

This principle of prayer should have been listed first in these principles, as it is the most vital and important factor in the success and growth of the church.

In the book, *FRESH WIND, FRESH FIRE,* Pastor Jim Cymbala writes, "PRAYER IS THE SOURCE of the Christian life, a Christian's life-line. Otherwise, it's like having a baby in your arms and dressing her up so cute—but she's not breathing! Never mind the frilly clothes; stabilize the child's vital signs. It does no good to talk to someone in a comatose state. That's why the great emphasis on teaching in today's churches is producing such limited results. Teaching is good only where there's life to be channeled. If the listeners are in a spiritual coma, what we're telling them may be fine and orthodox, but unfortunately, spiritual life cannot be taught.

"Pastors and churches have to get uncomfortable enough to say, 'We are not New Testament Christians if we don't have a prayer life.' This conviction makes us squirm a little, but how else will there be a breakthrough with God?

"If we truly think about what Acts 2:42 says—'They devoted themselves to the apostles' teaching and to the fellowship, to the breaking of bread and to prayer'—we can see that prayer is almost a proof of a church's normalcy. Calling on the name of the Lord is the fourth great hallmark in the list. If my church or your church isn't praying, we shouldn't be boasting in our orthodoxy or our Sunday morning attendance figures."[4]

Chapter Five

A PREPARED CHURCH

The Scripture we used from Acts chapter two says, *"They continued in the apostles doctrine."* They continued to prepare themselves and give themselves to the careful, prayerful study of the Word of God that they possessed and the teachings left to them from Jesus. I'm sure you would expect to read something like this from a college president. My burden and concern goes far beyond the fact that I have served as a college president. I have a deep burden for the preparation of people for works of ministry. I am not just speaking about the professional clergy. I dislike using the word "professional", but for the want of a better word to distinguish the professional clergy from the laity I use it. Let me emphasize again, and I will continue this emphasis, that all of us live under a divine mandate and we all have a divine call. I believe that we all need to recognize that call and respond to it in our service to God, and allow Him to manifest Himself through us in ministry through those gifts He has given us.

All believers are gifted people. Romans, chapter 12 says that "To everyone is given a measure of faith", and then lists seven powerful gifts that are given. I believe we are all gifted people and we need to discover and develop those gifts. That is not pride being manifested, but a consciousness of the fact that God has created us as unique, gifted individuals to be used for His glory.

I believe that if the church is going to grow in numbers we have to grow in the knowledge of the Word of God. We cannot grow without the Word of God. Any other growth is superficial and will not produce long-lasting results. We must discipline ourselves in preparation and teaching of the Word of God.

For several years I enjoyed a rather unique place in life where I was surrounded by hundreds of students every day who were preparing themselves for a life of service and leadership in a multitude of callings and fields and majors. I am so committed to, and such a believer in, higher Christian education. In a world where the principles of morality and the foundations of the Christian faith are being attacked and systematically destroyed, it is a joy to see young people ... and I shouldn't say young people as I shook the hand of a 67 year old graduate who walked across the stage to receive his diploma ... whose lives and education are being built on strong biblical principles.

My goal was that when the graduates left Northwest College they would go out into whatever profession God was calling and leading them to interpret the morning newspaper in the light of the Scripture, that every decision they make will be based on God's Word. Every decision that is made in life, whether it is family decisions, financial decisions, business decisions, church decisions, must be based on biblical principles.

If we do not do the preparing, I believe that we are going to jeopardize the future, not only of our country, but also of the church. I am concerned with some growing trends in my own denomination in the preparation for the clergy. There are some third-world developing countries that have stronger educational requirements for their clergy than we do. There is a demand being placed on them that they be prepared.

Please see with me the necessity of preparation. I want to go beyond the professional ministry that we might call "full-time workers", or "full-time ministry" because I think we are all full time. We are all in this business together, and though you may work at Boeing or Microsoft you are "full time" in serving Jesus. Your occupation just pays the bills because we are all full time in this business of serving Christ and being part of Kingdom business on this earth.

Let me leave a challenge to every fellowship and denomination. I share these thoughts out of great concern when I see the small percentage of our own church college students who even consider one of our Christian, church-sponsored-colleges. This should be a concern to every denomination. If we don't educate our young people, they are going to get an education some place. The generation that we call the "baby boomers" and now the "buster generation", the Gen-X's are the most highly educated group of people in the history of the world. They have grown up among us and now are establishing their families. If we do not educate our own children, they will get an education somewhere, and if we do not provide it for them, we will have a phenomenal brain-drain of leadership in the church.

That New Testament church was a prepared church. They were diligent in their preparation. When you go back and look at the leadership in that church, those people were highly qualified, intellectually and academically prepared for the leadership that God raised up in those days. Though God used some people who may not have had some of the opportunities of others, He called people who had a wonderful intellectual background and used them to inspire and teach others.

If you take the apostle Paul out of the New Testament you

don't have much left. The apostle Paul probably was one of the most highly educated people of his day. There wasn't anyone who had a finer education. He was a graduate of the University of Tarsus who had sat at the feet of Gamelial for his post-graduate work.

I'm old enough to have grown up hearing some of the old-timers say, "Bless God, I would rather hear an anointed preacher than an educated preacher." That was a regular statement I heard in my youth. Frankly, I would rather hear an anointed preacher than an educated preacher, but what I never heard anybody say was, "I'd really like to hear an anointed, educated preacher." That's what we need. I've heard people say, "Well, all you have to do is get up and open your mouth and the Lord will fill it." Unfortunately, I've heard some of that kind of preaching and their mouths got filled all right, but the Lord didn't do it. It was just a bunch of hot air and a waste of time for me and everybody else.

My Bible says to "study to show ourselves approved unto God, workmen who need not be ashamed, rightly dividing the word of truth." I've had some phenomenal times of anointing, but during those times it was not stuff that just came out of the "blue." It was thoughts that I had put away. I had studied, I had tucked away truths, I had listened carefully to others who were inspired by God, and the Holy Spirit brought it back to my remembrance and made it alive and renewed in my thinking. It is not scriptural (you will not find it in the Scripture) that you can get up and open your mouth and the Lord will fill it. That is not in the Bible. That experience was only reserved and promised for those who would be arrested for the cause of Christ and get thrown into jail and brought before the magistrate, the judge, the jury. And then it was promised that you don't have to worry … "at that time I will put words in your mouth" the Lord promised. Jesus promised that when He returned to the Father He would send the Holy Spirit who would bring back to our remembrance ... what? ... "the things that I have told you." The things that we have carefully received from the Word of God will come back to us in special moments.

I remember when I was a college student. It was test day and the professor asked a student to pray at the beginning of the class. The student prayed, "Dear God, I pray that you will bless us today and help us in this test. Please help us to remember the things that we have studied and help us to remember the things we haven't studied." That was an impossible request! God could never do that! It is a violation of Holy Scripture. He's not going to bless nothing. He's going to bless something that we have been diligent to put away.

I am dedicated to the integrating of faith and learning. I am committed to seeing values taught on the college level. I failed in the past as a pastor when some young person would come to me and say they couldn't afford to go to a Christian college. I would say, "Why don't you go to the community college? Why don't you go to the junior college? Get your basics out of the way and then go on to the Christian college." What a drastic mistake I made and what terrible counsel. I think the basics need to be taught in the framework of biblical truth and on a biblical foundation. If you can't afford a four-year education at a Christian college, go there and get your basics and then transfer somewhere else.

I have totally reversed myself from my previous thinking and counsel. If I had a student of my own today, they would go first of all to a college that will present truth in a biblical sense. I'm talking about sociology, English, psychology, philosophy, U.S. History, World History, that would all come from a Christian, biblical viewpoint.

I was sharing some of these thoughts in a conference, and when I finished a minister from my Fellowship came up to me and told me, "You don't have any idea how bad it is." He went on to say that he had graduated from one of our denominational colleges and had been credentialed in the ministry. He was doing post-graduate work at a state university. He told me, "One day I found myself sitting in class and the thought went through my mind, 'so what's so bad about being a homosexual? If that's your orientation, what difference does it make?'" He went on to say, "I had sat there day after day and hearing that material, having my faith and my morals attacked again and again, until all of a sudden I realized they almost had me."

One of my college president friends told of a young lady who had enrolled at their college. She was one of those who had thought she could go to the junior college and pick up her basic courses without the cost of a private college. On the first day in this junior college, in an English composition class (now how harmful can an English class be?) the professor entered the room to meet the class. He went to the board and wrote, "John is going to marry Nancy." Then he said to the class, "What does that statement mean?" A brave student raised his hand and said, "It means John and Mary have been dating. They have come to the conclusion that they are in love and they are going to get married." The professor said, "Wrong. It means that they are going to buy into an outmoded idea called marriage. It means that they think that they have to have a piece of paper to cohabit. And further, it means that they're not homosexuals. That's what that means." That absolutely amazed this particular young woman. She said, "Here I was, in the very first day of a class, and somebody is trying to destroy my morals and my value system." She got up from the class and went immediately to the Christian college where she was planning to attend later and enrolled.

A student came to me on our campus. He had enrolled in the university. On his first day in class a professor came in. He didn't know who the students were. He stood and said, "If any of you are carrying a Bible you can get rid of it today. That book has been proven to be outmoded hundreds of years ago." Here is a person who is attacking the Bible, a book that he undoubtedly has never read, and immediately intimidating any Christian student in that class.

I am only saying that the New Testament church is a prepared church. They were preparing themselves to properly present the teachings and life-style that Jesus Christ had left for them.

In a day when we are witnessing the rising of cults and non-biblical teaching it is imperative that we have a church (pastor/leader and people) who are well grounded in the Word of God. We are living in a day when there is teaching that is extra-biblical and doctrine that is based on experience rather than the Word. As that happens an individual is open to all types of non-scriptural teaching and behavior. Manifestations of the Spirit, and human responses can never supersede the clear written, inspired Word of God. The survival of the New Testament church perhaps, more than anything else, lay in the fact that they "continued steadfast in the apostles doctrine."

Chapter Six

A PREACHING CHURCH

Acts 8:1 *"On that day a great persecution broke out against the church at Jerusalem, and all except the apostles (the underlining mine) were scattered throughout Judea and Samaria.*

Acts 8:4 *"Those who had been scattered preached the word wherever they went."*

This New Testament church was a preaching church. We must never minimize the power of preaching. We read that those who had been scattered, preached the Word wherever they went. In Acts chapter four and verse four we read, "But many who heard the message believed and the number of men was about 5,000." What produced the great growth of 5,000 men coming to God? It was the preaching of the Word. Nothing will ever substitute for the preaching of the Word. We will never have legitimate and lasting growth without the preaching of the Word.

I was in a meeting, as a young evangelist, when a man stood during a testimony time and said, "I have just returned from down home (wherever that was). Since I have been gone for these past two months from this church I have been in wonderful services the whole time. In fact, I never heard the preacher preach one time. In every service the glory of God came into that place and the preacher didn't preach for the entire two months I've been gone." As a young, rather bold evangelist, I got up and said, "Brother, I don't know where you've been, but I will tell you this. If you have not heard the preaching, teaching of the Word of God in the last two months, you haven't grown spiritually." I was not impressed with his testimony.

We do not grow on manifestations. We grow on the Word of God. We have manifestations to inspire and encourage our hearts, but you do not grow on spiritual manifestation. You will grow by the consistent preaching, teaching of the Word of God. "Faith comes by hearing and hearing by the Word of God." It doesn't come by manifestation.

The power of the New Testament church lay in the fact that they were a preaching church, along with these other qualities.

It is interesting to note the content of their preaching. A good exercise is to read Peter's sermon he preached on the Day of Pentecost. It is not a long recording. Peter on that day did not preach about the baptism in the Holy Spirit and speaking in tongues. He had just witnessed this phenomena. He did not preach about divine healing. He did not preach about the second coming. He didn't preach about the rise of the anti-Christ. He preached about none of these things. He preached about Jesus Christ, the One they crucified and had risen from the dead. That was the heart of his sermon. And 3,000 of them responded to that sermon.

He came in the power of the Holy Spirit to preach about Jesus, and that is the message that the world needs to hear.

We have often majored on some doctrinal point. We get more interested in some point of doctrine rather than the fact that men and women are lost and need a Savior.

We need teaching. We need to involve ourselves in the teaching of the truths of God's Word. We must understand the foundational truths of our faith. But what the world is looking for is someone to help them meet the needs and demands of today, and to speak to the loneliness and emptiness of life. People are looking for reality. A person who has no relationship with Christ does not need to hear some unique doctrinal approach to the Scripture, but needs to be introduced to the Doctrine of Jesus Christ, the One who came to bring life in all of its fullness and abundance.

This was found scrawled on the wall of a theological seminary, "And Jesus said to them, 'who do you say that I am?' And they replied, 'You are the eschatological manifestation of the ground of our being, the *kerugma* in which we find the ultimate meaning of our inner-personal relationship.' And Jesus said, "What?'" This message about Jesus is not complicated! Go back and look at the messages Jesus preached. Little children could sit all day and listen to Him and not eat their lunch. It was a message of life, it was a message of hope, and it was a message where people lived and understood. It was a message that presented to them a new and better way to live.

During one of my trips to Brazil I went to participate in one of the State conventions of my church. While in the area I preached in one of their large churches and witnessed the phenomenal growth of that church. In my particular Fellowship we were talking and strategizing our plans and goals for the final decade of the twentieth century and the number of churches we hoped to start and the number of new Christians to be added to those churches. I learned that those people had started 1,500 churches the previous year in Brazil, and that they had 75,000 churches established in the country. I asked someone, "What is the secret of this explosive growth in Brazil. What is producing this revival?" The person shared with me an interesting insight. This brings me to my next principle.

Chapter Seven

A PARTICIPATING CHURCH

Acts 8:1,4 ... *"all ... were scattered ...preached the word wherever they went."*

Acts 8:14 "When the apostles in Jerusalem heard that Samara had accepted the word of God, they sent Peter and John to them."

On that particular trip to Brazil, to which I referred in the previous chapter, I inquired about the explosive growth of the church in that country. I was told that on the morning after a person received Christ as their Savior, they would go back to work and request a week's vacation. They would board a bus or train and go to their family and share their new faith. That family would become believers and the process would be repeated again and again.

I read of an account where Billy Graham was asked, "What is the secret of the South American revival?" And his answer was, "Everybody is a preacher."

Billy Graham was in South America for a series of meetings and one afternoon had been invited to go to a military armory to address the soldiers. On the way into the giant armory auditorium he saw a crowd of soldiers out in front. He made his way through the crowd and saw a soldier, standing on a box, preaching to the crowd of soldiers as they were on their way into the armory. As he got closer he looked and saw that there were four stars on the shoulder of the soldier's uniform. Here was a four-star general who was "preaching" to his men. Billy Graham stated that wherever he went, everyone was a preacher.

While in Brazil I was invited with some of the local leadership to visit a government official who was involved in the rewriting of the constitution for the nation. After our brief visit the man asked us if we would lay hands on him and pray that God would use and anoint him for his task. Here was another "preacher" working within the government.

There is a story we all love to tell during a mission convention and it has been in print and widely circulated, but illustrates so forcefully the power of communicating the Gospel to people. A young woman in Sao Paulo who was a prostitute, totally illiterate, and dying of social diseases because of her life style, came to an Assemblies of God church and was saved. She didn't know anything about God. She didn't know how to read. They gave her a little Bible, and she said, "Would you mark those Scriptures you gave me?" So they took her Bible and marked the Scriptures.

The next day she went out into her neighborhood and knocked on the door of a home and said, "Last night somebody gave me this book. I don't know how to read. Could you tell me what this says where they have underlined it?" She took them through the plan of salvation and gave her testimony, and before she left they gave their lives to Christ. Then she would go to the next door and would say, "Last night some people gave me this book…" and go through the same process again.

It wasn't long before she had 200 people gathering. She called the missionary and said, "Please send some help. I don't know what to do with these people. Send me a preacher." A simple, illiterate prostitute that Jesus had redeemed, transformed, and healed the night she received Christ had turned into a preacher. That is the spirit of the New Testament. Everywhere these people went they were preaching the Gospel.

That is one of the great principles of the New Testament, everyone was a minister. Everyone got caught up in the desire to fulfill what we know as "The Great Commission."

If the words of Jesus to "Go into all the world and preach the gospel" was directed only to the disciples and not to be the command to the entire church, then we can continue to let the professional clergy do it all. That word "preach" in the original text is the word, *euaggelizo*, our root word for evangelism. The passion of the new testament church was to evangelize everywhere in response to our Lord's command to *"not leave Jerusalem, but wait for the gift my Father promised ... but you will receive power when the Holy Spirit comes on you; and you will be my witnesses in Jerusalem, and in all Judea and Samaria and to the ends of the earth"* (Acts 1:4b, 8).

Today we have the New Testament principle that produced this powerful church all backward. The apostles (pastors) are scattering themselves everywhere while the laity is content to let them do all the work.

It was my privilege to become acquainted with Dr. Henry H. Ness, the founding president of Northwest College. My sister married his youngest son, Eugene. Dr. Ness was a man of tremendous vision and a great man of faith. He was one of the most austere men that a person could ever meet. I hear stories from former students who were at the college during his tenure. He would frighten them nearly to death with his stern approach. I had the opportunity as a young man to conduct a crusade for him while he was pastor in Oakland, California. He became a strong supporter of my ministry and a source of great encouragement.

One night Dr. Ness had retired for the night and received a call around the midnight hour. A lady who was a member of the church was on the phone and said, "Dr. Ness, would you please come down to the hospital? I'm down here and there's a man who is dying and he doesn't know Jesus. Would you please come down here and lead him to the Lord?" Dr. Ness said, "It's midnight." She said, "I know, but the man's dying." He said, "I'm in bed." She said, "Yes, I know, but the man's dying." He said, "It's cold outside." She said, "I know, but this man's dying and not expected to live until morning." He said, "Sister, how long have you been a Christian?" She replied, "Thirty years." He said, "You mean you've been a Christian for thirty years and you would call me up in the middle of the night and tell me a man's dying? Lead him to God yourself!" He hung up the phone and went back to sleep.

The next morning the lady called him and said, "Oh, Dr. Ness, I had the most wonderful night! I had the glorious privilege of leading that man to Jesus at two o-clock this morning. He had a great experience with God and he died at four o'clock, and went to be with Jesus." Why not! It's not the pastor's job to run around all night praying for people. It's everybody's job. We all have relationships we have nurtured and developed. These become our opportunities to minister.

I used to have people come to me as their pastor and say, "Would you please go call on my neighbor who is in the hospital?" I would ask, "Is the person a Christian?" They would reply, "I don't know." "Does he have a pastor?" "I don't have any idea." "Well," I would say, "Don't ask me to go visit them. You're the one they know." If I walk into that room I don't have any relationship with the patient. They don't know me. They resent the fact that somebody sent the preacher to them. But you see, when we have built relationships with people we become the New Testament "scattered" ones. They were the ones in the New Testament who were out doing the work of the ministry … "all except the apostles."

The church will be stymied, the church will not, cannot grow if the work of the ministry is confined to one individual. The work of the ministry cannot be confined to the pulpit alone. We all must be dispatched to this world by the power of the Holy Spirit to take the gospel everywhere as these people did.

It is extremely interesting to note who became the "preachers" in this New Testament church. When the "great persecution broke out against the church" every one scattered and preached the word … "all except the apostles." Where did we get this turned around in the church? When did we arrive at the "professional clergy/preachers" who run around everywhere and the majority of the church stay in their secure "Jerusalem"?

I am not minimizing the call to pulpit ministry, but neither am I excluding the call and mandate that every believer lives under to "go into all the world and preach the gospel to every creature."

I'm afraid that we have measured our evangelism by saying that teaching a Sunday school class, preaching sermons, serving on a board or committee, or singing in the choir is somehow equivalent to evangelism. That may be a ministry, but we cannot content ourselves with anything less than reaching lost souls with the message of the gospel.

This problem can go back in history to when these New Testament Christians had, in less than 300 years, completely undercut the pagan Roman Empire and had put a Christian Caesar upon the throne. People were taking the gospel everywhere and people were being converted. Then something awful happened. Constantine ended the persecution with an edict in 313 A.D. (that was not awful), but then sometime later Theodosis made another edict which made the whole world Christian and millions of people came into the church who were not evangelized and the church became a sort of "spectator sport" where they let "Clerical George" do it. It was given over to the professional clergy to do the work of evangelism.

The greatest heresy there is, and you may not read it in a book or have it listed in a study of false doctrine, is that laymen believe the minister is the one who fights all the spiritual battles for the souls and minds and hearts and bodies of individuals, and the task of the lay person is only to support the ministry. This means that since 99.5 percent of the church is non-clerical then 99.5 percent of the church is not "going everywhere preaching the word."

I have called what we are seeing today in the church, "the second reformation." When Martin Luther led the first reformation the Bible was released from the pulpit. Up to that time the Bible had been literally chained to the pulpit. Isn't it interesting that in the providence of God for the renewal of His Church that the Gutenberg printing press was developed in the same era as the coming of Martin Luther in his new-found discovery that "the just shall live by faith." It was only natural, after basically only read and interpreted by the priests, that when the Reformation occurred there was the release not only of the Bible from the pulpit, but the quantity of Scriptures became more available.

I have heard much criticism of the Roman Catholic Church stating they had prevented the people from any personal exposure to the Scriptures and the Church was the only vehicle for the dissemination of the Word. It was not so much a prevention from the people as it was, up to that time, a preservation of the Word. Naturally, a long tradition of the handling of the Scripture was not easy to change. It was revolutionary to the Church to think of the release of the Scripture into the hands of the common people, but that release through the proliferation of the availability of the printed page was one of the accompanying features of the Reformation.

In my short lifetime I am witnessing what I call, "The Second Reformation." We have seen the release of the Scripture to the people. Now we are seeing the release of ministry to the people. In my opinion we are getting back to what New Testament Christianity is all about. It has been too long that people have sat in church pews, coming to a building to be "fed." There are many pastors who are under great duress today endeavoring to "feed" people who are, for the most part, overly spiritually fed already. That criticism that "I am not being fed" is not heard from people who are involved in ministry. These people are so hungry to receive after giving of their own spiritual resources and participating in ministry and sharing their faith that they are hungry to "be fed." These are the ones who are easily satisfied and that hunger will always be met through the Word shared by faithful pastors who have diligently prepared themselves for their own responsibility as a shepherd/teacher.

The spirit of the New Testament is ... "DON'T KEEP THE FAITH ... PASS IT ON!"

The "preaching" church will see that become a reality.

Chapter Eight

A PAYING CHURCH

Acts 4:32-36 *"All the believers were one in heart and mind. No one claimed that any of his possessions was his own, but they shared everything they had. With great power the apostles continued to testify to the resurrection of the Lord Jesus, and much grace was upon them all. There were no needy persons among them. For from time to time those who owned lands or houses sold them, brought the money from the sales and put it at the apostles' feet, and it was distributed to anyone as he had need. Joseph, a Levite from Cyprus, whom the apostles called Barnabas (which means Son of Encouragement), sold a field he owned and brought the money and put it at the apostles' feet."*

There is no question, this was a paying church. They were givers. They brought everything they had and laid it at the apostles' feet. There may come a day when we will do that again. These people out of great persecution had all things in common. This church was not a model for communism, but rather an example of a caring fellowship of people who were vitally involved in each other's lives.

The biblical principle of giving precedes the law. There are critics today of the tithing principle who say we no longer live under the law. But this principle was part of God's plan long before the institution of the law. In Genesis 14 we read of the blessing Melchizedek, king of Salem, gave to Abram. Immediately following the blessing we read, "Then Abram gave him a tenth of everything." In Leviticus chapter 27:30, 32 the Lord says, *"A tithe of everything from the land, whether grain from the soil or fruit from the trees, belongs to the Lord; it is holy to the Lord. The entire tithe of the herd and flock every tenth animal that passes under the shepherd's rod—will be holy to the Lord."*

Jesus Christ said, *"Woe to you, teachers of the law and Pharisees, you hypocrites! You give a tenth of your spices— mint, dill and cummin. But you have neglected the more important matters of the law—justice, mercy and faithfulness. You should have practiced the latter, without neglecting the former"* (Matthew 23:23).

The Apostle Paul in his letter to the church at Corinth writes, *"Now about the collection for God's people: Do what I told the Galatian churches to do. On the first day of every week, each one of you should set aside a sum of money in keeping with his income, saving it up, so that when I come no collections will have to be made"* (I Corinthians 16-1-2).

Again Paul writing to the Corinthians, *"Remember this: Whoever sows sparingly will also reap sparingly, and whoever sows generously will also reap generously. Each man should give what he has decided in his heart to give, not reluctantly or under compulsion, for God loves a cheerful giver. And God is able to make all grace abound to you, so that in all things at all times, having all that you need, you will abound in every good work"* (2 Corinthians 9:6-8).

The Proverbs encourage us, *"Honor the Lord with your wealth, with the first fruits of all your crops; then your barns will be filled to overflowing, and your vats will brim over* with *new wine"* (Prov.3:9-10).

"One man gives freely, yet gains even more; another *withholds unduly, but comes to poverty. A generous man will* *prosper; he who refreshes others will himself be refreshed."* (Prov. 11:24-25).

In a book written by Cliff C., Jones, *Winning Through* *Integrity,* the author shares several illustrations and quotes from individuals who had discovered the value of following the biblical principles of tithing. Gordon Groth, former president of Electra Manufacturing Company, once said that he had known many regular churchgoers who, for one reason or another, quit going to church, but he had never found any people who stopped tithing once they had established the practice. His comment was that they were afraid to stop because their tithing had brought them increased material blessings, which they felt would disappear if they ever discontinued it.

Cliff Jones wrote of William Volker, the inventor of the roll-up window shade, who gave away enormous amounts of money. While still a comparatively young man, he was worth several million dollars. He and his wife decided they would keep one million and gave away all above that amount. His friend's thought he had lost is mind. One of those friends said to him later, "I was sure you would end up in a pauper's grave, but here you are, richer than ever, despite all the money you have been shoveling out for years."

William Volker replied, "Yes, I have been shoveling it out, but God has been shoveling more of it right back to me, and God has a bigger shovel."[5]

An acquaintance of mine was at a dinner meeting seated next to R. G. LeTourneau, the creator-industrialist of heavy equipment. Thinking he would get a good illustration on giving, he leaned over to Mr. LeTourneau and said, "Sir, I understand that you are a tither." LeTourneau answered, "You heard wrong. I am not a tither. I give ninety percent of my income to God and keep the other ten percent for my own living and personal expenses."

There are laws that govern and guide this universe that have been set in motion by our Creator/God. He is the One who established the laws of gravity and centrifugal force, not man. If I announced to you that I had reached some level of spirituality where I could now fly and invited you to come and watch me fly off the top of some high building, it would be a sad sight. No matter how spiritual I may claim, or profess to be, I would fall to the ground in a broken heap.

If I had an automobile that performed and handled well and could corner at high speeds, there would still be a limit on how fast I could maneuver through corners because there is the law of centrifugal force. There is a limit to how fast that car would travel through certain corners. When the speed exceeded the centrifugal force factor for that particular car on that particular corner, the car would roll off the road and crash. It would not depend on how well the car maneuvered or how good of a driver I was. The car would crash because there is a law of centrifugal force in operation.

One does not break the laws of God. We are the ones who become broken. The law of gravity was not broken by the leap off the building. The law of centrifugal force was not broken when the car went over the embankment. The individual was broken. The law remained intact.

It is the same with the law of giving and receiving. The Bible says, "Give and it shall be given unto you." That is as much a part of the laws God established in this universe as the laws of gravity and centrifugal force.

When my son was young, probably ten or eleven years of age, his mother was cleaning his room one day. She noticed on his dresser a ledger that he had developed. The simple ledger had three columns. The first column was headed,

"Income." In that column he had placed all the money that he got from little jobs. It seemed he was always making money mowing lawns, picking berries, running errands, etc. He included in that "income" column any money that he had received from gifts, also. The next column was headed, "tithe owed", ten percent of the first column entry. The third column was, "amount and date paid." His mother showed me the ledger.

A short time later I had opportunity to be with my son and said, "Your mother showed me your ledger. I want to commend you and let you know that you have already built the seeds of success into your life and whatever you feel that God wants you to do you cannot fail. Whatever you do you will be a success, because when you build your life on God's principles, you cannot fail."

Years later my son went away to college. I never assisted him financially, except to keep his car on my automobile insurance policy. He worked his way through college and then through graduate school.

As he was nearing the final days of his graduate school-work a new contemporary Christian radio station came on the air in Dallas, Texas. (He was attending school in Fort Worth.) They were conducting a contest to establish their listening audience and listeners were asked to submit their names for a drawing to receive prizes. The day of the drawing arrived. The grand prize was a trip for two on a Caribbean cruise. Jeff, my son, was listening to the radio and the grand prize was drawn. The name drawn was a college classmate and now a seminary classmate of his. Jeff ran to the phone and called his friend who was not listening to the radio. The prize had to be claimed within a certain number of minutes or they would draw another name. Jeff's friend, Mark, called the station and won the prize. The day after graduating from seminary these two young single men left FortWorth to go on a Caribbean cruise.

I said to my son, "This is just God's way of blessing you for your hard work and discipline in getting through school, and for your faithfulness in your personal giving through the years." I believe that to be a fact.

Please don't tithe to receive a Caribbean cruise, but when you are faithful to God He will bless you and will meet your needs. That I believe.

I realize that our motivation for giving is not getting; however, when you live according to God's immutable laws, you will reap the results. You can't stop God from blessing you.

Preachers often use the text, "Whatsoever a man soweth, that shall he also reap" in a negative connotation. That verse of Scripture has both a negative and positive declaration. If you sow righteousness, you will reap righteousness, just as surely as if you sow evil you will reap evil.

In Malachi 3:8 and 9 we read, *"Will a man rob God? Yet you rob me. But you ask, 'How do we rob you?' In tithes and offerings. You are under a curse—the whole nation of you—because you are robbing me."*

Then that wonderful promise appears in verse 10, *"'Bring the whole tithe into the storehouse, that there may be food in my house. Test me in this,' says the Lord Almighty, 'and see if I will not throw open the floodgates of heaven and pour out so much blessing that you will not have room enough for it.'"*

God is challenging us to put Him to the test and prove Him.

As a leader in the church I would never allow anyone to assume a place of responsibility who was not a tither. In my opinion, that individual is a dangerous person. They cannot be trusted. I would not want to live next door to them. I would be afraid they would siphon the gas out of my car at night, or they would steal my lawnmower if the garage door was left open. Why not? If they would steal from Almighty God, why wouldn't they steal from someone like me?

One of the curses of Christianity in the Western World is

that we have not known how to use our blessings. There has never been a society of people who have been blessed more than those who are living in North America. We will be held in great accountability on the Day of Judgment on how we used those resources trusted to us by God. A promotion on the job or a raise in pay has been used as an indicator that it is time to move to a bigger house, buy a boat, put a barbecue in the backyard, go on some exotic vacation, or some other materialistic expression. It so often never occurs to us that God has entrusted finances to us to enhance His Kingdom.

In our church we had no more than concluded our World Outreach Week where "Faith Promises" had been received for our missions budget for the next year, when a lady approached me. She said, "A wonderful thing has happened to my husband and me. We unexpectedly inherited some money. My husband has told me that we can use that money to buy new furniture and redecorate the house." I said to her, "Has it ever occurred to you that God may have blessed you so that you could bless a lost and hurting world?"

I strongly believe in the tithing principle, but there comes a time in our lives as God blesses us that to only be a tither is not being responsible in our stewardship. For many years my wife and I have given a double tithe. We have set giving goals in our lives. This is not a bondage to us, it is a joy. I am more concerned about fulfilling my goals and obligations to God than I am for other needs. By handling our personal finances in a responsible manner we have been able to give more. We have never accumulated consumer debt and never have paid a dollar of interest on credit cards. Yes, we have credit cards that we use for personal convenience, but we have always paid the balance off by the due date.

The Proverbs give us a lot of advice on how to handle our finances. I would recommend that you read those proverbs every day. The book is conveniently divided into 31 chapters, one for every day of the month. I read some of those proverbs every day. There is a promise of wisdom that comes from reading that book in the Bible. The Proverbs say, *"It is possible to give away and become richer! It is also possible to hold on too tightly and lose everything. Yes, the liberal man shall be rich! By watering others, he waters himself."* ... *"Trust in your money and down you go! Trust in God and flourish as a* tree" Proverbs 11:24, 25 and 28 (The Living Bible)!

Chapter Nine

A PURPOSEFUL CHURCH

Acts 2:38 Peter replied, *"Repent and be baptized,
every one of you, in the name of Jesus Christ so
that your sins may be forgiven."*

It is rather difficult, in the interest of selecting a reference
from Scripture, to find a single verse, or passage in the
Book of Acts to point to the purpose of this New Testament
church. By even casual reading of the Book you will quickly
discover that the motivation of those involved was to introduce and win people to Jesus Christ. That theme runs
throughout the entire narrative.

I am convinced that a church can never grow or enjoy any
lasting success without a clearly defined statement of purpose. If a church does know who they are, why they exist,
who they are trying to impress/reach, their motivation for
ministry, they will revert to being nothing more than a social
club, a meeting place for those who are part of the established group, and nothing more. Dr. James O. Davis in a
communication with me stated, "Our purpose determines
our programs, our programs design our procedures, our procedures determine our policies, our policies direct our peo-

ple, our people develop our product."

Once you establish your identity then everything you do must support that statement of mission and purpose. Believe me, it has to be communicated clearly and regularly.

Our statement of purpose that we established in Salem, Oregon where I served for twenty years was:

"THE PEOPLE'S CHURCH ... a fellowship of caring people, developing toward maturity, being equipped to live a positive Christian life, reaching out to others in non-judgmental love." (Acts 2:41-47)

This statement was used as a bookmark that was made available to everyone to be used in his or her Bible. It was regularly part of our display advertising in the newspaper. It appeared on our giving envelopes. We talked about it. Let's analyze what that statement says. First, we are just people. Second, we are people who genuinely care for people. Third, we are not perfect. We are developing, but we have not arrived. It was often communicated that we are all on some rung of the ladder that is reaching toward maturity and none of us have arrived at the top. If you want to come and get on the first rung, you are welcome, because we are all in some process of growth and development in our Christian life. Fourth, we will present the gospel in a positive way. We will minister to the needs of people, but we are not going to dwell on negativism. We are not going to criticize and find fault. We are committed to presenting Christ and the abundant life He promised in an attractive way. Fifth, we are going to accept everyone into this fellowship. We are not going to judge people on where they came from, their lifestyle, their current living conditions, but take them where they are and point them to this exciting life that Jesus provides.

I am convinced that people are looking for something more in life than what they have found through materialism, pleasure, notoriety, and sensual pursuits. I have never felt it was my duty to bring people under condemnation. Jesus said, "The world is condemned already" and that He did not condemn to them. If that is true, and we believe that it is, then our privilege is to share with the world that they don't have to live as they are, but there is something more to life and it is found in Jesus.

A man, whom I had never seen before, greeted me at the front door following a Sunday service. He said, "I would like to teach in your church." I replied, "I would suggest that you get into The Pastor's Class (a class conducted every Sunday for new people to the church) and find out what this church is all about and our philosophy of ministry." He said, "I believe in the hard gospel." I responded, "I'm not sure I know what that is. I believe in the 'good news.'" I never saw the man again. Undoubtedly the purpose of our church would not meet his interpretation of what the gospel is all about.

Dr. Robert Schuller told us one day how to handle a negative thinker. He said you handled them like you handle a wolf out in the wilds. You can take a club and beat them to death. They might eat your leg off while you are doing it, but if you swing hard enough and long enough with the club you will ultimately kill them. Or, you can just build a great big fire and don't put any food out and the wolf will slink off into the brush and leave you alone.

That to me is by far the best way to handle a negative thinker … just build a great big, positive fire, and don't put out any negative food for them, and they will slink off into the brush and leave you alone.

People are wanting to know how to live. Our purpose is to point them to that kind of life.

When a statement of purpose is established it then becomes the motivation of every group within the church to design all of their activities to support that statement.

We were committed to reach our entire city for Christ. It is the height of arrogance to believe that somehow you are the only church in town, or that there are not others who are just as committed to Christ and the lost as you are. I believe in a cooperative spirit. I believe in supporting other churches in their efforts to reach a community. However, there is a danger in cooperation. The danger becomes a negative force when we somehow reduce our efforts with the thought that someone else is going to be reaching part of a city for Christ. When that becomes our attitude, we lose our focus.

I had not been in Salem very long when one Sunday our District Superintendent dropped into a worship service, unannounced. I asked him to greet the congregation. In his remarks he extended congratulations for the great growth he had witnessed and the success the church was enjoying. We had doubled in attendance in the past few months. When he finished his comments, I jettisoned to the pulpit and said, "Brother Superintendent, I don't appreciate what you just said. We are not successful. This church will never be a success until everyone in this city comes to know Christ." That is what I wanted that congregation to feel. Yes, we need to feel good about ourselves and what we are accomplishing, but we must never lose sight of the enormity of the task before us and strangle on some momentary success.

I was asked to speak to all of the ministers in our city on the subject of church growth. I shared with them some of the principles we were practicing. When I finished I expressed my deep appreciation for the privilege to be working in the same city with them. I confessed my love for them and the privilege to be brothers in the ministry. I told them how much I admired what they were doing, but that when I walked out of that door I was going back to my "mission field" and that I was not counting on them to win that city. That was my responsibility and I, though I loved and respected them, was going to forget they were there. I pled with them to do the same toward me that when they left that room and went back out into that city that the burden of their hearts would be, "If this city is going to be won to Christ and impacted by the gospel, it is up to me." That is the way we all must live.

When a church has a clearly defined mission statement, that must be communicated when there is a change of pastoral leadership. Unfortunately, church boards fail in their selection process of a new pastor to communicate the mission of the church. They are often looking for strong leadership, but it is extremely important that new leadership carefully ascertain the mission of the church. The work of God is put into reversal at times when insecure leadership comes and moves a church from a long standing, God blessed ministry, to a totally new approach. I have seen some great churches lose their influence in a community and never recover.

Mission statements can be refined and changed, just like a constitution and by-laws. But, these refinements must never lose the heart of the original mission. I feel great sorrow today for churches that are being jerked around by people who are off on some new approach or style and lose their moorings. It is a pity to see pastors who go off to a conference and come home with the new idea of the month. We are terrible imitators. We need to be motivators. We must hear what God has for our particular place of ministry.

Years ago Doug Wead, who later became a part of the George H. W. Bush administration as a liaison from the president's office to the evangelical church community, came to speak in the church where I pastored. This was not Doug's first or last time to minister there. He was involved at the time with the Charismatic Movement around the world. He had been an integral part of the Vatican Council and the Catholic Charismatic Movement. At that time he said to me, "Don't let the Charismatics push you around. You do what God told you to do. You keep focused on what you are doing now. God is blessing it."

Years later Doug came back for another series of meetings. He asked me, "Do you remember what I told you years ago in regard to the Charismatic Movement?" I replied, "I never forgot it." He said, "Well, you took my advice. You remained faithful to what you felt God wanted you to do. You didn't detour from your philosophy of ministry and outreach." He went on to say, "The Charismatic Movement has gone full circle. They are back today exactly where you are and always have been. You stuck to your guns and built this great church. You won."

People are looking for consistency today. That does not mean we should never change. We have to change if we are going to survive in areas of life or business, but there are some things that never change.

Youth for Christ had a motto, attributed to Billy Graham, perhaps they still do, which said, "We are geared to the times, but we're anchored to the Rock." I like that. We must move with the times. We must make changes, but the heart of our message and our philosophy of ministry and reaching the world will never change.

I understand that in the Kellogg museum in Battlecreek, Michigan, there is a room that you are taken to where you are shown the evolution of the Corn Flakes. On the wall is the first box that Corn Flakes were sold in and the demonstration goes on to show all the boxes down to the current box on the shelves in today's markets. The guide says, "The corn flakes you ate this morning are the same corn flakes your grandmother ate, but we package them differently today, and that is all."

That should be the goal of the church. The product does not change, but the packaging must to meet the needs of the day and to be presented in an attractive and relevant way.

Rick Warren's book, THE PURPOSE DRIVEN CHURCH, published by Zondervan, is absolute must reading on this subject. The by-line to the title of this book is, "Growth Without Compromising Your Message & Mission."

Chapter Ten

A PURE CHURCH

Acts 5:13-14 *"No one else dared join them, even though they were highly regarded by the people. Nevertheless, more and more men and women believed in the Lord and were added to their number."*

In the King James Version an interesting word is used for the phrase "more and more men and women believed" which reads, " ... multitudes both of men and women" which would indicate that significant numbers of people were being added to the church.

The interesting thing about this continued growth and addition to the church is that this reporting of "multitudes", "more and more men and women" being added to the number, immediately follows the tragic account of Ananias and his wife Sapphira, who were both stricken dead because of their deceit regarding the gift they were giving to the church through the sale of a piece of property.

After Ananias fell down and died we read that "great fear seized all who heard what had happened." It is interesting that this report did not hinder the growth of the church, but seemed to enhance it.

The message to the church and to the unbelieving world was that this was a "pure" church and there were serious consequences of belonging to this church and uniting with this group of people.

Do we take seriously enough what it means to belong to the Church of Jesus Christ? We are often encouraged at the time of the receiving of the Holy Communion that we are to examine ourselves. The words of the Apostle Paul are read ... *"A man ought to examine himself before he eats of the bread and drinks of the cup. For anyone who eats and drinks without recognizing the body of the Lord eats and drinks judgment on himself. That is why many among you are weak and sick, and a number of you have fallen asleep"* (I Corinthians 11:28-30).

I am aware that what occurred in the New Testament Church as it related to Ananias and Sapphira is not the normative occurrence in a church service. However, Paul's warning to the church at Corinth carries some serious connotations. I have seen several examples of the Ananias and Sapphira principle being repeated in my own experience. I continue to see that occurring. It is painful to watch. I am convinced I have witnessed premature deaths, illnesses and tragedies that are a direct result to "not properly discerning the Lord's body." That body being addressed in this scripture, in my interpretation, is not the physical body of Christ hanging on a cross, but rather the body of Christ that now makes up His Church.

I have heard this Scripture used at the time of communion in a warning to non-believers not to participate and partake of the communion elements. This warning was not given to non-believers, but to those who had identified as part of the church, the body of Christ. I have often said that if a non-believer comes in and participates of the communion all he is doing is wasting the bread and ingredients in the cup, but it has no negative effect upon the individual. However, it is quite a different situation of the one who claims to be part of the body of Christ and then takes lightly that association and relationship.

Loving Pastor Peter suddenly turned into a man of steel as he faced the lying Ananias. If these times for discipline occur in the church, we need to support spiritual leadership as tough, legitimate situations are faced. I'm not talking here of some whim created by leadership when they may not feel that they are receiving the proper support of some personal agenda, but validated violations of unscriptural behavior.

I have read of that great Philadelphia Church in Stockholm, Sweden, which served for so many years as an example for many of us. I heard of an instance where a church member had to be disciplined for action that was unbecoming and unacceptable for an individual who held membership in the church. It was a closed meeting, meaning that only members were in attendance. When the announcement that this person had been dealt with and continued to live in open sin, there was nothing left to do at the moment but to dismiss this individual from membership. When the announcement was made it was reported that the entire church immediately fell on their knees and begin to intercede in prayer for the restoration of this fallen member. That is a spiritual church.

It reminds me of an instance in my own ministry. There was a neighboring pastor of another denomination who was being greatly used by God as a powerful voice for the evangelical churches in our area. I had befriended this pastor. He had phoned me on Tuesday and asked me to go golfing with him. To my regret, I told him I was too busy. He had said that he needed to visit with me about a young man who had been part of our church at one time. I have looked back on this situation with a great degree of personal pain for my insensitivity to what was undoubtedly a cry for help.

Two days later I received a call from a pastor of yet another denomination asking me if I had read the evening newspaper. It was still on my front porch and had not been brought into the house. I went out and retrieved it and opened it to read of a terrible tragedy that had occurred in my city of an immoral activity that named and included my pastor friend who had phoned me and wanted to be with me. I was devastated.

The following Sunday as people were leaving the church, after this news had been carried daily in the newspaper, individuals would come by me at the door and say, "Pastor, we've been praying for you" or "Pastor, we know that this has been a tough week for you." The following Wednesday evening I said to the congregation, "A great tragedy has befallen our community and the church. There is no need to hide our heads in the sand to the fact of this terrible situation." I then read from Galatians, chapter six, which says, *"Brothers, if someone is caught in a sin, you who are spiritual should restore him gently. But watch yourself, or you also may be tempted."* I said, "That could have been your pastor, but for the grace of God."

As I talked further suddenly the entire church fell on their knees and began to pray for this fallen brother. The hurt and pain I felt due to the situation was still there, but I went home that evening rejoicing in the fact that I was part of a spiritual church that reached out in love, not to condone sin, but to love and pray for a fallen brother.

In the midst of the tragic account of Ananias and Sapphira I believe you will find that this New Testament church was a fellowship of people who were quick to restore. In fact, it seems that the Apostle Paul had to come down on the church at Corinth because they were tolerating immoral behavior in the church and allowing someone to participate who clearly was living a life that was a detriment to the testimony of Jesus Christ and the church.

In our desire to have a "pure" church, it is absolutely essential that New Testament practice and discipline be followed. All of us in places of spiritual leadership have had to deal with situations that were extremely unpleasant. The New Testament is quite clear in the process of such discipline. Let me say that when a person needs to be publicly disciplined, this should always be in the context of a "closed" members only meeting. These are not occasions for this type of church business to be conducted in a public meeting. The word will get around that it is serious business to belong to the church of Jesus Christ.

One of the benefits of having a standard for membership is to hold up the integrity of the church before an unbelieving world. There have been times when I have been approached by people outside the church who asked me if a certain person was a member of the church. I could tell that the question came because of some unscrupulous business dealing or some kind of behavior that was not becoming to a Christian. It was always a comfort to be able to respond that the person in question was not a member of the church, though they might be an attendee. This always seemed to satisfy the one who was asking.

It is interesting that the world outside the church often has a higher standard for us who are part of the church than we do for ourselves who are in the church.

Any church has the privilege of establishing their standards for membership. This is difficult for some to understand. I endeavor to explain the difference between biblical absolutes, personal convictions, and community standards. They are all unique.

I remember as a young pastor that there was a minister in our state who never wore a tie, which was very proper and fashionable to do in some circles. He always wore a white shirt, buttoned to the top. He was always neat and well groomed. I never heard him condemn anyone for wearing a tie, but undoubtedly he had a personal conviction that wearing a tie was worldly. I respected that older gentleman. I always looked at him as a man who lived by his personal convictions. He had no Bible absolute for not wearing a tie, nor was there a community standard restricting this type of dress. But he had a personal conviction. Let's honor that kind of conviction. On the other hand, when we do not agree with some community standard, let us honor that standard as long as we are part of that particular community. I think if a person is honest in their relationship with that community and searching for a spirit of unity they will quietly leave if they cannot honestly support the standards of the particular group of which they are a part.

Chapter Eleven

A PERSECUTED CHURCH

Acts 8:1 *"... On that day a great persecution broke out against the church at Jerusalem ..."*

This portion of Scripture immediately follows the account of the stoning of Stephen and the persecution that was being led and fueled by Saul of Tarsus.

It seems that persecution has been part of the history of the church. We in the western world have been extremely blessed and privileged not to have had to live under the cruel and severe persecution that so much of the rest of the world has suffered.

In the earlier days of this century we had a few tomatoes and rotten eggs thrown at the church building, an occasional rock thrown through a window, and perhaps a few hecklers. But, can we call that persecution? A man who served on the college board of directors where I served told me how his pastor/father who served in Spokane, Washington, was tarred and feathered and run out of town eighty years ago. In our day of tolerance nothing quite that traumatic would occur except in very rare instances.

There are many areas of the world that have suffered

severe persecution during this century. Persecution has never seemed to diminish the growth of the church, but at times has appeared to enhance it. In 1948, when persecution began in China and all missionaries were expelled, they left behind approximately 50,000 Christians. Persecution grew to horrendous proportions during the Cultural Revolution. It was amazing how they seemly obliterated Christianity from the culture.

I went to Shanghai, China in 1983 when tourists were just beginning to gain entrance. The people still all wore the traditional gray clothing. There was very little color. Our presence in the country put us under a considerable amount of surveillance and suspicion. At that time the population of Shanghai was approximately eleven million. There were only eleven churches open. They were all Three Self Churches who were licensed by the government. When the western church was allowed greater access we discovered that the church had prospered, unrecognized and often underground, quite well. When our missionaries left the 50,000 Christians behind in 1948 it was now discovered that there were 100 million Christians in China. Persecution will never destroy the church.

After receiving communication from a certain area of the world, we called our students to prayer for a pastor who had been sentenced to die after having been in prison for nine years. In the call that came to pray it was stated that "he does not want the church worldwide to pray for his release or for the commutation of his sentence, but simply that God's will be accomplished, whether by his life or his death." Miraculously he was spared at that time through a foreign delegation that happened to be traveling through the country, and the government did not want to be embarrassed by this incident. Unfortunately, the Bishop that was communicating with the church in the west was later ambushed and assassinated.

Martyrdom is not a unique experience of previous centuries, but it is reported that there were more martyrs for Christ in the twentieth-century than any other century in history.

The unknown poet wrote:

On the far reef the breakers recoil in shattered
*   foam;*
Yet still the sea behind them urges its forces
*   home;*
Its chant of triumph surges through all the
*   thunderous din,*
The wave may break in failure but the tide is sure
*   to win.*

O mighty sea, thy message in changing spray is
*   cast:*
Within God's plan of progress it matters not at
*   last,*
How wide the shores of evil, how strong the reefs
*   of sin;*
The wave may be defeated but the tide is sure to
*   win.*

One thing remains forever sure, the Church of Jesus Christ will triumph. The gates of hell will never prevail against that church.

We often hear the reports of those who have suffered greatly for the cause of Christ and question our own strength and ability to ever stand in such a time. We can be comforted by the promise that assures us "that as our days are, so shall our strength be." When we read the accounts of Corrie ten Boom and her sister, Betsy, being tortured by the Nazi's and read their accounts of the presence of God, we can take courage. I remember reading the account of the night Betsy and Corrie were taken by the German soldiers out into the sub-zero weather with nothing on but thin cotton dresses to freeze to death. They were placed in this "freezing furnace" to die. Corrie ten Boom said, "While we were out there Jesus came and stood with us. I would speak, Betsy would speak, and then Jesus would speak. The soldiers who were dressed in thermal gear were punished when the next morning they brought the young ladies back without even a hint of frostbite. The commanding officers knew that they must have done something to protect these young women.

Brigadier General Robinson Risner, who spent seven and a half years in Vietnam as a prisoner of war, and a great deal of that time in solitary confinement, told me one day that sometimes he missed being in that prison because Jesus was so real to him there. He shared with me how God would come and talk to him in an audible voice. One day after his release and his assignment to the air base outside Las Vegas, Nevada, he was traveling into the city from the base to speak at a noon luncheon. He prayed in his car and asked, "God, why aren't you as close to me now as You were when I was in Vietnam?" He told me he heard the voice of God again, which was the last time he heard God speak to him, when He said, "You don't need me now in the same dimension that you needed me when you were in Vietnam."

Those accounts encouraged me to know that whatever I am going through, God will meet my at the place of my need with the grace and strength to endure.

Chapter Twelve

A PRAISING CHURCH

Acts 21:47 *"praising God and enjoying the favor of all the people."*

One of the distinguishing marks of the New Testament Church is joy. This New Testament Church was a praising, joyful church. I have often said that joy and the Holy Spirit are first cousins. You can't have the filling of the Holy Spirit without at the same time being filled with joy. Anything other than that is a contradiction.

There is the misconception that joy is always accompanied by some happy feeling. The joy the New Testament talks about goes far deeper than feeling.

A few years ago there was a great emphasis placed on praise. So much of what was written on the subject at the time was sound, but there were those who went overboard on the subject. They emphasized that you were supposed to praise God "for all things." The Bible doesn't say we are "to praise God for all things", but we are to "praise God **in** all things." There is a vast difference in those two statements. During those days of extreme teaching on the subject people were encouraged to praise God for cancer, to praise God for an adulterous husband or wife, to praise God for their children's wayward lifestyle. We are not encouraged to praise God for all things, but in all things.

In John, chapter 15, Jesus is talking about the relationship we have with the Heavenly Father and in verse 11 He says, *"I have told you this so that my joy may be in you and that your joy may be complete."* This word joy in the original means just what it says. The word is *khar-ah'*, which means, "cheerfulness, i.e. calm delight:—gladness, be exceeding joyful." If you have access to an exhaustive concordance, look up this word and the many references throughout the New Testament where the word is used.

This promise of joy supersedes our circumstances. The joy that Jesus possessed certainly was not dependent on the results of His ministry, the faith of His friends, the impending death He faced, but went far deeper than those earthly disappointments, pain and problems.

We sang a little chorus that said, "They will know we are Christians by our love." That is true, but they will also know we are Christians by our joy. A joyless Christian is a contradiction to the Christ we profess.

I heard of a little boy who grew up in a very strict home. (I grew up in a strict home, also, but nothing like the home I am about to describe.) When Sunday came they were to keep the total day "holy." After church and Sunday dinner the children were not allowed to go out and play because they were to keep this day holy. One particular Sunday afternoon the little boy was fidgety and wanting to be outside until his father finally said, "You can go out, but remember this is the Lord's Day. Don't run and play. Remember what day this is."

As the little guy walked out the back door of the farm house he saw a little calf romping around the pasture and he said to himself, "That's too bad that our calf is not a Christian." He walked into the barn and saw their new little kittens wrestling and playing in the hay and he said, "What a shame. All of our new little kittens and to think they are going to hell." Then he looked across the barn and there standing in its stall was the old mule. Its face was long and its eyes were watering. The little boy looked at him and said, "Now, there is a real Christian."

That's what the world thinks about a lot of us. The happiest people in town ought to be the Christians. When we are out in public the unbelieving world should be able to say, "There is another of those happy Christians."

My father pioneered/planted a church when I was just a small boy. There was a man who had been driving some distance to church, who along with his family joined this fledging group. He operated several logging trucks and was one of those happy, optimistic persons who was an attraction to others. He had a non-Christian neighbor who was just the opposite. He also was a log truck owner. No one ever did anything to suit him. The ones who loaded his truck always, according to him, either loaded it with logs too long, too short, not enough, too many, or some other thing that would solicit a complaint from him.

His Christian neighbor had been sharing his faith and inviting him to church. One day the Christian lost one of his trucks. As the truck was coming out of the mountains with a load of logs, the brakes failed. The driver of the truck bailed out and the truck went off the road and down into a canyon. The pessimistic, sour-puss neighbor saw the wreckage and got home that evening before his Christian neighbor. He stationed himself in his house where he could see out of the window facing the Christian's house. He said to himself, "I'm going to see how Christian takes all of this."

Before too long a truck dropped the Christian neighbor off right in front of the non-Christians house. As he got out of the truck and begin to walk up the long driveway leading to his house, the non-Christian could hear him whistling, swinging his lunch pail, walking with a spring in his step as if he had enjoyed the best day of his life. That was too much. The non-Christian came to church the following Sunday with his wife and three teen-age children. The parents gave their lives to Christ in the morning service and the three children that evening. Those were the first converts in my father's ministry and that church. Why? Because there was a Christian who was "filled with joy and the Holy Ghost."

If our unbelieving world cannot see any difference in our reaction to the sorrows, setbacks, disappointments and pain of life, why should they get excited about this Christ we profess can change our total outlook on life?

The Psalmist said, *"I will bless the Lord at all times. His praise shall continually be in my mouth."* Our lives should be lived in an attitude of praise. Praise will blow the dark clouds of doubt and depression from one's life.

Chaplain Merlin R. Carothers in his book, *Prison To Praise,* shares the account of a young military couple and their response to the husband's orders to go to Vietnam. Ron, the young soldier came to see the chaplain and told him he had to help him. His wife had tried to commit suicide when he had been drafted into the army. The chaplain asked him to have his wife come to see him.

When she came in she expressed her fears. She was trembling from head to foot and tears flowed uncontrollably down her face. The chaplain felt such compassion for her that tears came to his eyes. The chaplain prayed silently for a word to say to her. He felt the Lord say to him to tell her to be thankful. He couldn't believe that he was hearing from God.

The details of the young woman's life and her need for security is far too much to share. However, after much travail both of them begin to thank God in this situation. Sue, the young wife, finally had the strength to pray: "God, I thank You that Ron is going to Vietnam. You know how much I will miss him. You know I don't have a father or mother or bother or sister or family of any kind. I will trust You Lord."

Ron had prayed: "God, I do thank You. I give Sue over to You. She is Yours and I'll trust You to take care of her."

After they had prayed that prayer in the chapel, Ron went back to his duty. Sue went into the waiting room outside the chaplain's office. A young man came in who needed counseling. It turned out that this young man was Sue's brother who she didn't know existed. Chaplain Carothers asks, "There are more than two-hundred million people in the United States. What would be the odds against that particular soldier walking into the door to my office just as Sue had made a covenant with God to praise Him for her loneliness and lack of family."

That was not all. As Ron walked back into his unit, he ran into an old friend from law school who was now a legal officer. When asked where he was going and he reported that he was on his way to Vietnam, the friend persuaded him to ask for a transfer so that he could work with him in the legal office. The request was granted and the young couple did not have to be separated.

The chaplain says, "The very act of praise releases the power of God into a set of circumstances and enables God to change them if this is His design."[6]

Arthur Bingaman wrote:

> *When clouds seem thick around you and troubles*
> *seem to drown you.*
> *Praise the Lord.*
> *When you suffer grief or pain and you've prayed*
> *in Jesus name, beloved,*
> *Praise the Lord.*
> *When your prayer brings no relief from your*
> *agony and grief:*

Praise the Lord.
When someone says things that offend, remember
*   this my friend:*
Praise the Lord.
When troubles come in like a flood, remember
*   you are under the blood:*
Praise the Lord.
When it rains or when it shines, when folks are
*   mean or when they're kind,*
Praise the Lord.
When life goes into reverse and things get worse
*   and worse;*
Praise the Lord.
When you feel so blue you don't know what to do,
Praise the Lord.
Beloved, don't give way to tears, anxieties and
*   fears:*
Praise the Lord.
Look up in Jesus' face. He will give you more
*   grace:*
Praise the Lord.
When it seems you cannot stand, just hold onto
*   Jesus' hand, and*
Praise the Lord.
Life will be sweet if you kneel at Jesus' feet, and
Praise the Lord.
When tribulations comes, do not try to run, just
Praise the Lord.
You will be so content with whatever He has
*   sent, if you*
Praise the Lord.
You will be happily surprised how far away
*   Satan flies, when you*
Praise the Lord.
He won't hang around, for he doesn't like the

sound, when you
Praise the Lord.
It is an expression of love to our Lord above,
    when we
Praise the Lord.

We must not underestimate the value of praise. There is a little formula in I Thessalonians found in three short verses: "Rejoice ever more. Pray without ceasing. In everything give thanks." Every prayer time should include those three elements. A lot of our praying is only asking for a lot of things. We do very little praising, very little thanksgiving. Asking is only one dimension of prayer. We need to rejoice. We need to give thanks. Our prayers should be accompanied with praise. So, let's join that New Testament church and praise the Lord!

Chapter Thirteen

A POWERFUL CHURCH

Acts 1:8 *"But you will receive power when the Holy Spirit comes on you ..."*

That promise was certainly fulfilled in the lives of those who identified themselves with this New Testament church. That power was manifested in a variety of ways. However you might identify the experience they received on the Day of Pentecost, it was certainly a life-changing event in the lives of these followers of the now resurrected and ascended Christ.

It seems that wherever they went this enduement of power was felt. It did not matter if it was before the Sanhedrin, in a Roman or Philippian jail, standing before a Caesar, walking down the street and having your shadow fall on a person, courage to stand for the truth, or willingness to face opposition and death to identify oneself with these followers of Jesus.

We often translate power into some kind of "noise" or outward expression or manifestation. The noise of the water going over the dam is not the power. The power is generated inside the dam, and the noise of the water going over the spillway is just the overflow of what has already been produced.

This "power" in the New Testament church was demonstrated in changed lives. It was reported by unbelievers that these people who received this power had "been with Jesus." This "power" had an attractiveness about it that created a desire in the hearts of those who came in contact with it that they had to receive it, or at least they were impacted by it.

This powerful church of the first century brought such a change to their world that they were accused of "turning the world upside down." This power was not translated into demonstrations against the government or social system, but in transformed lives. When lives are transformed by the power of the gospel, there will be change. There will be political and social change. These become natural outflows of genuine, spiritual change.

We must never forget that the great challenges we face today will never be remedied by the passing of laws or political change. Our great need is to see the hearts of men and women changed by the power of God. This power is available for us today as much as ever.

This church had such power that on one day over 3,000 were added to their number. Another account reports that 5,000 were added, along with reports of "multitudes" and "a great number" becoming a part of this group, which indicates that power was being manifested.

We recall the account of Simon, the man who had practiced sorcery in Samaria, who saw the demonstrations of God's power and became a follower of Philip, the evangelist. Acts, chapter eight, records how this man, Simon, had elevated himself before the people with magic that had amazed them for a long time. Now he came in contact with a superior power. After witnessing the miraculous healings in Philip's meetings, he now came into contact with Peter and John who had arrived from Jerusalem. When he witnessed the power of the Holy Spirit he offered them money for the ability to lay hands on people to receive the Holy Spirit.

Peter's response to his request was that the gift of God cannot be purchased with money. Oh, that people today would be so attracted to the power of God that they would not err in thinking that this power could be purchased with money. Simon no doubt realized that this power would be an attraction to the world. What he had previously been able to do under the power of the "evil one" was now being supplanted and surpassed by this "new" power of God.

There is a power today that can change the hearts and minds of men and women. I heard Dr. E. V. Hill describe it in these words, "There is a power that can turn enemies into footstools and stumbling blocks into stepping stones. There is a power that can change harlots into missionaries. There is a power than can turn cursing and swearing men into gospel preachers. There is power than can open Red Seas and furnish manna from on high. There is a power that can cause walls to fall by marching around them and shouting for victory. That power is available for us today."

There should be a spirit of expectation that the miracles of God will occur in our lives and ministry. Often, in our desire not to exploit man, there have been miracles occur that we probably didn't give God the proper recognition for. I know that in my personal desire not to have attention drawn away from God and have someone say, "Denny Davis prayed for me and I got healed," I have endeavored to have others join me in prayer for special needs. I have an expectation that God is going to answer our prayer, and I want it known that it was God who did the work, not us.

I am very supportive of Christian counseling and have been involved in a Christian college where one of our strong majors was in the area of Behavioral Science. However, I believe there are some people who have come to depend on a counselor when what they need is to get to Jesus. There are times when people need to understand and see where the root of their problems may have derived. But Jesus is still the answer to our needs and He can do what no counselor, what no preacher, what no friend can do. We do need the support of one another, but we need to get to the all-powerful Jesus.

I had a young mother come to my office one day. She and her husband had two children of their own and they had adopted two other children. One of their little adopted children, four years old, was causing all kinds of confusion in the home. This mother was beside herself. She said, "That child is driving wedges between the children and even between my husband and me." The situation was critical. I learned later (not at that session) that it had become so bad that one night the little girl was told by her father to "Clean up your plate or you can't get down from the table," and she refused to do. So they got into a stand-off. Neither would back down. Finally the little girl cleaned the food off her plate, put it in her mouth, but in her stubbornness would not swallow it. The father was so frustrated that while giving her a bath, sometime later, pushed her head under the water. She gulped and the food was swallowed. That's how bad the situation had become.

That part of the story the mother did not tell me. She was only pouring out her heart about this child. I don't have the ability to counsel four-year-olds. I didn't have an answer for this mother. Finally I just said, "Let's pray." She said, "I don't have any faith that anything is going to change." I said, "That's fine, just sit there then and I'll pray." I offered a prayer. I didn't feel that she was involved in my prayer at all.

When I got through with my prayer I said to her, "Where are you going?" She replied, "I'm going home." I said, "That's fine. When you get in your car, don't turn on the radio. On your way across town to your home, just praise the Lord and say, 'Thank you Lord that you heard that prayer.'

You don't have to thank God for the answer, just thank Him that He heard because the God who hears also answers." She promised to do that.

That evening when the father came home from work, he told me later, "When I pulled into the driveway I felt something. I felt a calmness and peace that I had not sensed in days." As he was getting out of the car, the front door flew open and out ran this little girl. She grabbed him around the knees, gave him a big hug, and the problem was all over. No counselor did that. Our powerful God somehow got into the heart of that little child, and by the power of the Holy Spirit she was changed. That's the power I am talking about.

Chapter Fourteen

A PROGRESSIVE CHURCH

The Book of Acts concludes with the statement …
"For two whole years Paul stayed there in his own
rented house and welcomed all who came to see
him" (Acts 28:30).

I have two observations regarding Paul's activities that are
recorded here. First, he did not limit his activities though
in all probability he was living under "house arrest."
Secondly, he was accepting of all people.

Most commentators are of the opinion that Paul had limited amount of freedom and movement during these particular days. It is generally assumed that there were assigned
soldiers to guard him during this extended period of time.
Some have suggested that many of these guards must have
come to a saving knowledge of Jesus Christ through his
influence and witness.

Paul's attitude certainly discredits those who would
excuse themselves from spiritual activity due to some physical or geographic limitation. He did not let his confinement
stop him from serving God where he was. I have been privileged to know those who have suffered the loss of strength
through age or illness yet continued to find meaningful service. Some did that through prayer, others through writing

letters. It is always encouraging to see people who do not complain over their problems, but rather take those situations and use them to be an opportunity for service.

We see that this New Testament church was an inclusive fellowship and not exclusive. "All" were welcomed there.. They welcomed everybody into that church. Nobody was at the door checking their credentials.

I was ministering in another country where you had to show your membership card to get into their communion service. I was invited one Sunday to preach for this communion service. I'd been there for other preaching assignments. That day I climbed sixty three steps up a long stairway into the auditorium. There was one elevator available for the less energetic. I wondered if anyone would make their way up to this auditorium on top of this building. To my surprise there were probably 1,600 people jammed into the place. As I approached the door, one of the deacons was there checking everyone's card. He jokingly asked my host in his native language, "Do we check his card?" They laughed and I went on through the door and asked, "What did he say?" My friend said, "He asked if he should check your card to see if you are a member." That is an exclusive fellowship! You have to have the card!

We, in the Fellowship to which I belong, don't practice "closed" communion. I realize at times as a guest in another country and culture you need to adapt yourself to where you are.

However, those cultures might have greater response to meeting the needs of people if they were not so exclusive.

Our opportunities today are greater than they have ever been to reach our culture, our generation, with the gospel. The needs of our society are causing people to reexamine their own priorities. The "boomers" and the "busters" growing up among us are looking for values for their children. They are looking to the church for answers. If we can communicate the gospel in understandable terms and not major in pleasing ourselves, there is no end to what can be accomplished.

I was on a tour through the State of Oregon visiting the pastors in our denomination. I made thirteen stops and was pleased that 85 percent of the senior pastors of our 200 churches were in attendance. Traveling with me was a missionary from our state. During his second presentation he made a statement, "Before we can go to the mission field, there are two things we have to do. We have to learn the language and we have to study the culture. We are not permitted to go if we do not understand the culture of where we are going and if we don't know how to speak to them when we get there."

He went on to say, "I believe it is time the American church took cultural studies and language studies because no longer are we part of mainstream America. If you think we are living in Christian America, you have been asleep a long time and perhaps you need to wake up. We are now living in post-Christian America."

This is not all bad. When I was a young minister you would ask somebody, "Are you a Christian?" And they would reply, "Yes, I am. My grandfather was a Methodist preacher and we have been Methodists all of our lives." Or they might reply, "Yes, I was baptized into the church as a baby and I am a Christian." Or someone else might say, "I certainly am a Christian. I am an American and this is a Christian nation and everyone in America is a Christian.

That does not happen today. We are now two and three, sometimes four, generations removed from the church where people have no church contact from their parents or grandparents. In some ways it is easier today to present the claims of Christ than it was in earlier days. The lines are pretty clearly drawn. It is becoming increasingly more defined. When someone is asked today, "Are you a

Christian?" they often respond, "No, I'm sorry, I'm really not." Perhaps their opinion of Christians has been tainted by some people, or activities, by those who claim to be Christians. But the world is seeing the difference. In that sense the job of presenting Christ is made easier.

If we will talk the language that people speak and present the message in understandable terms, I believe we will witness an unbelievable response. That takes a commitment from all involved in a local church, both in ministry and as participants. So much of our activities and worship is centered around those who are already part of the church. Much of our worship is ego-centered. We as Christians want something that makes us feel good. Too many times we are not thinking about if we are communicating to those who come to be with us, let alone how we are communicating to God. I have described so much of what we call worship as nothing more than self-gratification.

We have many spiritual "hedonists" in our churches. A hedonist is someone who is seeking to be engaged in activities that make them feel good. When we come to worship God our purpose is not to feel good, but to make the heart of God feel good. Nothing makes God feel better than to see people come to know Him through faith in Jesus Christ.

One of my denominational leaders gave me the following dialogue which I also saw used with a group of college students in a skit. I'm sure it is in print, but it illustrates my point on communication.

ED: Have you ever been saved?

BOB: (A rather wide-eyed young man startled me with his question. He handed me a booklet with a picture of hell on the front.) Sure, once when I was nine years old. I was swimming at Jones Beach on Long Island. A strong undertow began dragging me out to sea and my uncle heard me cry out for help.

ED: No, no, no! Not that kind of saved. Redeemed! Have

you ever been redeemed? Reborn! Washed in the Blood!

BOB: What in the world are you talking about?

ED: Convicted! Have you ever been convicted?

BOB: Of course not! I've never been in trouble with the law.

ED: (Looking at Bob squarely in the eyes.) I think you need to be delivered.

BOB: Delivered? I was just sitting here waiting for a friend to pick me up. I think I will stick with that. Thank you very much. (Ed looked at me as if I was talking in another language.)

ED: Can we have lunch together sometime? I just work out in the streets.

BOB: Sure. That would be just fine. (He looked harmless enough but I must admit that he was an unusual fellow, quite difficult to understand.)

That Wednesday, Bob had lunch with Ed and he was a little late, but he explained that he was having some "quiet time."

BOB: Quiet time? What do you mean?

ED: Well, each day, just before lunch, I have some prayer in my prayer closet.

BOB: You pray in a closet? At work?

ED: No, in my car.

BOB: You've got a closet in your car? (He changed the subject like the first day I met him. Again, he left me confused. This fellow Ed is a unique fellow, I thought.)

As they parted that day, Ed gave Bob a little booklet that explained how a person can come into a relationship with God through Jesus Christ. Bob read it, reread it, and read it again. Finally, he began to understand that this was exactly what he really needed. That night, Bob committed his life to Jesus Christ and was born again as it said in that booklet.

Two days later, Bob told Ed about it. He was overjoyed! The following week they got together again.

ED: You need to find a good body.

BOB: (I was surprised at his suggestion. As far as I was concerned, it sounded just great! I took his advice and started calling the local health clubs for an attractive woman. There I met Denise. She had a good body and I knew she was the right one. We began to date and soon she became a believer, too.)

Ed rejoiced, and told Bob and Denise that it was critical they get planted so that they could grow together.

Bob confided to Denise that sometimes it was hard for him to understand Ed.

BOB: I didn't quite understand what you meant by "planted."

ED: Committed . . . committed! Now, that is what you both need.

BOB: Now, wait a minute. Just because I don't know what planted means doesn't mean that I'm nuts anyway. I don't need to be committed. I think that trusting in Jesus is the most sane thing I've done in my whole life.

It was obvious that Ed's patience was growing thin.

ED: Bob, you and Denise need to get plugged in. Do you understand?

BOB: (No, we didn't but I did wonder if getting plugged in had any connection with "going under the power" . . . something I heard Ed mention. I hoped that it would never come up again. Regretfully, I had to miss worship the next Sunday, but Ed didn't. I had breakfast with him the next morning and he filled me in with what had happened.)

ED: God moved.

BOB: He did? Where is He now? I was just getting to know him and now He's gone.

ED: No, no, no! God hasn't gone anywhere.

BOB: (I was relieved.)

ED: It was just that so many people were stepping out and moving in the gifts.

BOB: You mean that people were leaving in the middle of the service? And what about all of those presents?

ED: No, the gifts were really flowing.

BOB: That's beautiful. People were giving gifts to one another? I wish I had been there.

ED: Anyway . . . (changing the subject) Denise was there and maybe you heard about it. She was on fire.

BOB: Fire? Denise? Got burned? Is she okay?

ED: No, Bob, you don't understand. Denise is just fine. It's just that I believe that she got called and that God wants to use her. (Things aren't getting any clearer.)

BOB: Did Denise mention that she's getting too many phone calls? What is this that God's wanting to take advantage of her?

ED: (Sighed) Can I walk in the light with you?

BOB: Of course, we can walk in the light. It's still daylight.

ED: (Just shook his head.)

BOB: (Says to himself: I don't know what it is, but sometimes it seems that Ed and I have a hard time communicating.)

BOB: (speaking to everyone) Well I've been plugged in for two years since I was saved and delivered. Now, I am plugged in. I've been planted and committed to a good body. God has been moving and I've been stepping out in the gifts. I can't believe how God has been using me.

I've developed a new problem, it seems. My old friends don't understand me anymore. When I share about redemption, they don't understand that I've been washed white as snow and that I desire to follow the Lamb. They just seem to tune me out. I guess that they're just convicted because I'm on fire.

That's the way we talk. We are communicating in a language that is totally foreign to our culture.

One Sunday morning I was giving the invitation at the

close of the message and I used the word "justification." I publicly apologized. I said, "Please forgive me. We don't use that kind of language here." What I was saying to those who needed Christ was that I didn't expect them to know some of our theological jargon. I was also communicating to the members of the church, "You can bring your friends here who need to know Christ and we will present the message in understandable terms." When we begin to conduct ourselves and our services with that purpose, we will begin to see greater numbers of visitors and our members responding in bringing those who need to know Christ.

Too often, without realizing what we are doing, we become an exclusive fellowship. On one of my preaching assignments I arrived for the worship service early and found a seat in the front of the auditorium. My wife found a seat in the vacant sanctuary. In a few minutes a woman stopped at the end of the row where she was seated and walked over to her and sat down. In a theatrical whisper she said to herself, "George is really going to be upset about this." In a few minutes her husband arrived and sat down next to her. She said to him, in a voice loud enough for my wife to hear, "Well, George, it looks like we lost our seat today." Later in the service something was said that caused her to realize she was sitting next to the speaker's wife. She leaned over and said, "Honey, I'm sorry for the way I acted."

Let me ask you, what if my wife had been a visitor in that church that day? What if she had come to find help in a moment of desperation? Undoubtedly, she would have never returned and probably been so turned-off with the reception she received that it would have been extremely difficult to ever reach her again.

We were visiting in a distant city one weekend and decided to visit a church we had heard about. When we arrived there was not one person in the lobby. Someone finally came hurrying through and we asked, "Is there a class that we could attend this morning?" The person said, "Go down those stairs and you should find something down there." We proceeded down the stairs and saw people scurrying back and forth in the hallway. We stopped another person and asked the same question. We were told, "Go in there. I think you would enjoy that class." We entered and sat down. No one spoke to us. The teacher arrived and said to the class, after some introductory remarks, "Let's stand and greet each other." They did. They stood and greeted each other. Not one of them spoke to us. Before we ever had an opportunity to hear the pastor speak we were already turned off by the church.

In our congregation I often told the ushers, parking lot attendants, information center personnel, and lobby greeters that they were the most important people in the church. If people were not properly treated and received by them there was nothing I could do to remedy that later.

There are subtle messages we can give to let folks know that this is an "inclusive fellowship." I was speaking in one church that had sand receptacles at the front door for people to extinguish their cigarettes. That spoke a powerful message of acceptance. It said, "We want your kind here. You are welcome in this place." These are the people who need us. They are the ones for whom Christ died.

We often get the feeling that the sign in front of the church, the newspaper advertisement, the brochure mailed out will bring people in. Those are important, but a personal invitation is still by far the best and most effective means of attracting people.

One evening Nancy and I were eating in our favorite restaurant. The young proprietor, who was our friend, came by our table and said, "We'd like to get our girls in Sunday school." Their girls were probably six and eight years of age and had never been to Sunday school. Nancy said, "Oh, we'd love that." Then he asked, "What happens next after you come through the front door of the church?"

Here was a young businessman who was meeting people all day who came through the doors of his establishment, but was anxious about what a person would do who walked through the door of a church. Nancy assured him that if he would call she would personally be there to meet him and direct them to the proper place.

Church is a totally foreign place to the majority of our population. They would like to come. They acknowledge that the church is providing the help and assistance they need. However, they are hesitant to come because they do not want to be embarrassed or are afraid to invade a new environment.

Many people seem to think that if we identify with our culture in the interest of communicating with them that we somehow enter a compromising situation. The Apostle Paul was able to sense his audience and relate to his culture. He was not playing the part of a hypocrite when he said, "I have become all things to all men that I might win some." That's not hypocritical. Flowing with the culture does not mean that we have to change our convictions. It doesn't mean we change our doctrinal beliefs. It just means we might change our style a little so we can be all things to all people.

I was asked to assist in a funeral for a family that had distanced themselves from the church. Another minister was asked to bring the message. A few months later another member of the family died. They again contacted me and asked me to conduct the funeral. They said, "We don't want that other hell-fire and brimstone minister to conduct the funeral." That other minister had not been "hell-fire and brimstone" in his comments. He said nothing offensive to my understanding, but he did not identify with his audience and had offended them by his delivery style. To me it was unfortunate that he had been misunderstood and also that he was unable to change his style to identify with those to

A Progressive Church

whom he was asked to minister.

It was my privilege, serving as the Executive Director of Robert Schuller Ministry to Ministers, to have included in my area of responsibility the executive oversight of the Fuqua International School of Christian Communications at the Crystal Cathedral in Garden Grove, California. This "preaching school" was established in the early 90's in an attempt to meet the needs of established ministers/pastors who may have received some of the mechanics of sermonizing and homiletics, but that had never been taught the practical approach of communicating with an audience. The school is built around "The Four 'M's'", which are: The Messenger (who we are); The Message (what we say and how we organize and prepare our material); The Method (how we present it); and, The Milieu (to whom we are saying it). One of our assignments in the Advanced Session of the Milieu is to have the students present three messages, which are video taped during the sessions. All of these messages are built on the same Scriptural base. One is to be presented to a group of established Christians, believers, church-goers. The Second is to be presented to an audience of "seekers", those who know little, or nothing about the faith. The Third is to be delivered to a totally secular audience, or at least an audience who would be predominately secular. We encourage them to think in terms of speaking to a service club audience where you would not know if the people had any faith, or perhaps were from different religions. That is our challenge in communicating with our culture today.

We need to have leadership brainstorming sessions on how we can be a more "inclusive" church, and to identify those areas of exclusivity that are keeping people from this kind of fellowship.

Change is extremely painful. I know. I also know that without change we cannot progress and be what God wants us to be in our contemporary world.

When I was in the process of going through a change in my life, moving from a twenty year pastorate to become district superintendent, I was going through the pain of change. Knowing that I might be asked to serve in this position, I had gone away with my wife for a few days vacation. On our way home I was sitting by myself on the plane. (We're both stubborn and want aisles seats and were sitting across the aisle from each other.) Nancy was engaged in a conversation with a talkative seatmate. I was quietly praying, hoping to hear God speak to me and give me some direction regarding my future. My purpose in our vacation was to give God an opportunity to speak to me. I had received no special sense of His direction.

As I was quiet and pensive, I felt like I heard God say to me, "If you try to save your life, you will lose it, but if you will lose what you love so dearly (the church I pastored) you'll save it." At that moment I resigned myself to the will of God.

That is not to say that I did not suffer some pains of withdrawal and separation. One morning during the two and one-half month period after I had announced my resignation and before I left, I went into our staff meeting. The staff pastor who had been assigned the devotional time read the Scripture... *"As an eagle stirreth up her nest, fluttereth over her young, spreadeth abroad her wings, taketh them, beareth them on her wings: So the Lord alone did lead him and there was no strange god with him. He made him ride on the high places of the earth, that he might eat the increase of the fields..."* (Deuteronomy 32:11-13 KJV).

God used that passage to speak to me. We want to stay in our nest. It is safe there. Our needs are met and we feel comfortable in familiar surroundings. But, if we want to enjoy the "increase of the field" and soar into the high places, we must get out of our nest. It's frightening out there.

Do you see the picture portrayed in the Scripture? The mother eagle comes and pushes the little chicks out and off the high precipice. They begin to flutter and squawk. All they can see are the rocks below and the impending doom. At the last moment the mother eagle comes and swoops them up and carries them back to the edge of the nest. They breathe a sigh of relief and say, "I'm glad that's over." The mother eagle says, "It's not over. We're just beginning." It is not long before they master the art of flying and soaring and join the other majestic occupants of the sky.

If we are not willing to change we will miss out on the blessings and victories that God has planned for us.

Don Corbin, Field Director for Africa in the Division of Foreign Missions for the Assemblies of God, was sharing at a session I attended. He brought a message on "Holy Dissonance." He left these four comments that are so pertinent regarding our calling to be creators and perpetuators of holy dissonance:

1. Cutting-edge living and ministry cuts across the grain of the status quo. It creates dissonance between the ideal, God's anticipated outcome, and where we are.
2. Dissonance produces either evaluation and correction or defensiveness and self-protection.
3. The greater the comfort of the status quo, the greater loneliness of the creators dissonance. The prophets and the remnants of the Old and New Testaments were not popular people.
4. Creators of dissonance must determine to live in the discomfort of the reaction they bring. If they do not, they too will be overcome with the discomfort and succumb.

What a challenging statement! We have witnessed leadership through the years who have been so beaten up in their desire to bring positive change that they finally succumb because the discomfort level got too high. They either succumbed to the discomfort and return to the realm of the status quo or they give up and quit. What a tragedy!

Chapter Fifteen

A PERCEPTIVE CHURCH

===============

Acts 2:22, 32, 33 *"Men of Israel, listen to this: Jesus of Nazareth was a man accredited by God to you by miracles, wonders and signs, which God did among you through him, as you yourselves know. 32 God has raised this Jesus to life, and we are all witnesses of the fact. 33 Exalted to the right hand of God, he has received from the Father the promised Holy Spirit and has poured out what you now see and hear."*

This church knew who God is. It is amazing to me that with the little knowledge they had of the Scripture, and especially as we know it today, they had a clear theology and doctrine of God worked out. We might ask ourselves, "What is our concept and definition of God?"

It is absolutely imperative that we know who God is. If we are to survive today with all the winds, fads and trends that would even come through the church, we must have an understanding of who God is or we are going to get blown away.

With all the pain and disappointments that come to all of

our lives, if we don't understand the workings of a God who is eternal and who sees the future better than we see this moment, we will be disillusioned and be quick to turn our backs on God.

There is a humorous story in II Kings, chapter 6. In verses eight through thirteen it is recorded that the king of Aram was at war with Israel. After conferring with his officers, he said, "I will set up my camp in such and such a place." The man of God sent word to the king of Israel: "Beware of passing that place, because the Arameans are going down there." So the king of Israel checked on the place indicated by the man of God. Time and again Elisha warned the king, so that he was on his guard in such places. This enraged the king of Aram. He summoned his officers and demanded of them, "Will you not tell me which of us is on the side of the king of Israel?" "None of us, my lord the king," said one of his officers, "but Elisha, the prophet who is in Israel, tells the king of Israel the very words you speak in your bedroom." "Go, find out where he is," the king ordered, "so I can send men and capture him." The report came back: "He is in Dothan."

Please note the place ... "he is in Dothan."

If you have read this entire passage you remember what happened in Dothan. Elisha's co-worker, his servant, his traveling companion, or whatever the duties of this young man might have been, went out of the house to perhaps get a breath of fresh air. He looked and saw an army with horses and chariots surrounding the city. He went back in the house and reported it to Elisha and asked, "What shall we do?" Elisha told him that those who were with them were greater than those who were with the enemy. He prayed that the Lord would open his eyes so he could see. When he looked again he saw the hills full of horses and chariots of fire all around them. The Bible goes on to record the miraculous deliverance of Elisha and the city. The sovereign, miraculous God came to Dothan and did this great thing.

Back in Genesis chapter 37, you will recall how Joseph's father sent him out to find his brothers. He went to Shechem because that is where he heard they were. When he got to Shechem and couldn't find them he was told they had gone to Dothan. This is the same Dothan where Elisha had experienced God's great deliverance.

He found them at Dothan and you know the rest of the story. They took Joseph and put him in a pit. Ultimately they sold him as a slave and he was taken to Egypt. He was placed in a prison for years. Now, where is God? I thought God would come to Dothan and send horses and fiery chariots and angels to take care of those who loved him. Here is a young man who is pure in heart as proved by his lifestyle and the quality of his character. Where is God now at Dothan?

Our sovereign God does things that are unexplainable. Many times when we have a "Joseph experience" at our Dothan, somebody will come and say, "He didn't have enough faith. That's why this has happened." Or, "There must be sin in his life, that's why God is punishing him." Joseph had faith, he had vision, and he had not sinned. This young man was pure. He proved that in his relationship to Potiphar's wife who had tried to seduce him. That is what put him in prison. So you see, we cannot say that somebody does not know God properly, or that they don't have enough faith, or that they have sin in their life.

Our God works in ways we often cannot understand at the time. There may be times we are miraculously delivered and other times we will go through the pits even as Joseph did. We need to know this about God.

The same God who delivered Elisha is the same God who did not deliver Joseph. God had a plan and purpose that He was accomplishing through Joseph. Through a series of miracles, Joseph moved into a position of great power in Egypt and became the monitor of the food distribution during a time of great famine. So it was through Joseph that the nation of Israel and his family were saved during this famine. Joseph was the savior of the family from which Jesus ultimately came. That family would have died of starvation if God had delivered Joseph at Dothan, but God had a bigger and better idea, and God saved him. When his brothers came through the food lines and finally recognized whom they were dealing with, they were fearful of what he would to do them in retaliation. Joseph, in one of the great lines of the Bible, said, "Don't be afraid. You meant it for evil, but God meant it for good." We need to know this God.

We will never understand all there is to know about God. I don't think eternity is going to reveal everything about God to us. To me, that is what is exciting about heaven. We can spend eternity with God and will never know the fullness of who He is. I believe heaven will be a growing, learning, expanding experience.

To me the worst thing about hell is not the pain and the flame and the torture or even the loneliness. The worst thing about hell is the monotony. After you have been there for 24 hours you will have felt it all, seen it all, smelled it all, experienced it all, only to have an eternal rerun. But heaven will be a glorious adventure. Something new every day. This great Creator God is still creating. We will be involved in whatever He is doing.

I was asked once by the American Cancer Society in my city if I would be the moderator for a one-day seminar they were conducting. I know very little about cancer, but agreed to assist them. They brought in some of the oncologists who served in our city along with other medical personnel who were working with the terminally ill. The principle speaker that day was a Ph.D. from Berkeley, California. He had recovered from terminal cancer.

All of the participants for the seminar were having a lunch

together just before the meeting started. Someone at the table asked the special guest, "Doctor, did prayer have anything to do with your recovery and were you visited by any members of the clergy?" He answered, "No, I don't believe in that stuff. I suppose if you believe in it you could be helped by it." If he had concluded his remarks there I would have remained silent. But he continued, "And furthermore let me tell you why I don't like Christians. They are always living for the pie in the sky in the by and by, and doing nothing today."

That was too much for me. I said, "Dr. (calling him by his name), I want to tell you why I am a Christian. I am packing every day I have to the max. I end every day with a feeling of frustration because I don't have a few more hours. But, I keep my sanity because I know that I have a tomorrow. I've read in the last book of the Bible that those who know God are going to have the glorious privilege of being involved in his creative processes throughout all eternity. (My loose interpretation of the verse in the Revelation that says, "And the saints serve him day and night.") That's why I am a Christian."

At the end of the day, with a bit of cynicism in his voice, yet I felt with a great deal of respect, he came up to me and said, "You're a real pro at this stuff, aren't you?" I replied, "No, I just wanted to be helpful. The American Cancer Society asked me if I would moderate for the seminar and I was happy to do that."

You know what I think? I think the Holy Spirit got through to this doctor that day. It wouldn't surprise me to look over my shoulder when we are standing before the eternal throne of our Christ and see him there because one day he heard that there is more to life than what you can see right now. There is more to life than beating cancer…there is a God who has a tomorrow that goes far beyond anything we can know or experience today.

Do you know Him?

Eight year old Danny Dutton, who lives in Chula Vista, California had an assignment to write an essay on God. Here is what he wrote:

One of God's main jobs is making people. He makes these to put in place of the ones that dies, so there will be enough people to take care of things here on earth. He doesn't make grown-ups. Just babies. I think because they are smaller and easier to make. That way he doesn't have to take up valuable time teaching them to talk and walk. He can just leave that up to mothers and fathers. I think it works out pretty good.

God's second most important job is listening to prayers. An awful lot of this goes on as some people, like preachers, pray other times besides bedtime. God doesn't have time to listen to the radio or TV on account of this. As he hears everything, not only prayers, there must be a terrible lot of noise going on in His ears, unless he has thought of a way to turn it off.

God sees everything and hears everything and is everywhere which keeps him pretty busy. So you shouldn't go wasting his time by going over your parents' head and ask for something they say you couldn't have.

Atheists are people who don't believe in God. I don't think there are any in Chula Vista ... at least there aren't who come to church.

Jesus is God's son. He used to do all the hard work, like walking on water, doing miracles and trying to teach people about God who didn't want to learn. They finally got tired of his preaching to them and they crucified him.

But he was good and kind like his father, and he told his father they didn't know what they were doing and to forgive them and God said O.K. His father appreciated everything he had done and all his hard work on earth, so he told him he didn't have to go out on the road anymore. He could stay in heaven—so he did. And now he helps his father out by listening to prayers and seeing which things are important for God to take care of and which ones he can take care of himself without having to bother God ...like a secretary, only more important, of course. You can pray any time you want and they are sure to hear you because they've got it worked out so one of them is on duty all the time.

You should always go to Sunday school because it makes God happy, and if there is anyone you want to make happy, it is God. Don't skip Sunday school to do something you think will be more fun, like going to the beach. That is wrong. And besides, the sun doesn't come out at the beach until noon. If you don't believe in God, besides being an atheist, you will be very lonely because your parents can't go with you everywhere, like to camp, but God can. It's good to know he is around when you are scared of the dark or when you can't swim very good and you get thrown in real deep water by big kids. But you shouldn't just always think of what God can do for you. I figure God put me here and He can take me back anytime He pleases. And that's why I believe in God .

I like Danny's theology. How is yours? We need to understand the nature of God; His spirituality, His personality, His unity, His revelation through the Trinity. We need to know the attributes of God; His omniscience, His omnipotence, His omnipresence, His eternalness. We need to understand his moral attributes; His holiness, His righteousness, His faithfulness, His mercy, His love.

This growing, thriving, world-impacting church in the New Testament knew who God is. With the proper understanding of God you can face a lot of difficulties and opposition. You can go through a lot of pain, because you know the eternal workings of God and that there is a divine purpose. A church will never grow and lead people to a place of maturity without knowing who God is.

Chapter Sixteen

A PATERNAL CHURCH

In Acts, chapter sixteen, is the account of Paul and Silas being held in prison when a violent earthquake occurs that causes the prison doors to fly open and the chains come loose from the prisoners. The jailer was so distressed that he was about to commit suicide when Paul shouted to him that he should not harm himself because the prisoners were all there. He fell before Paul and Silas and asked them what he must do to be saved. Vs. 31 records their words to the jailer, *"Believe in the Lord Jesus, and you will be saved—you and your household."*

God is interested in families. God works on "the family plan." It is His will that families be united in Him. God's desire is to be the head of every home. What a difference that makes in all relationships within the family.

Leaders within the church have a particular responsibility to model a Christian home. We must keep our priorities in proper perspective. I let everyone who joined the church I pastored know that the local church did not have a higher priority in my life than my family.

When my son was entering his senior year in high school I announced to my church board, and then to the entire congregation, that I was going to spend thirty days with him during that year. Really, that was not a great commitment. That was only every other Saturday. I made this public announcement for two reasons. I wanted to place myself under an obligation to fulfill my commitment, but I also wanted my son to hear his father publicly state that he was a high priority in my life. I had to work hard at it that year. I took him with me on some out-of-town engagements to fulfill my number of days that I had committed, but we had a wonderful year as a family.

I had a deacon come to me once and say, "I know we have a board meeting scheduled, but my son is playing basketball that night. Do you think it would be all right if I missed the board meeting and went to see my son play?" I replied, "You shouldn't be at the board meeting if your son is playing basketball. There will be a lot of board meetings, but you will have very limited opportunities to support your son like that."

The church went on, and today, many years later, that father and son have a wonderful relationship. That boy grew up to be a son who honored his family and today is serving the Lord in a missionary ministry. His father had, and still has, a strong spiritual influence upon him. That influence might have been diminished if that father had not had his priorities right.

There is nothing more effective in a person's ministry than to see his/her family serving the Lord.

I am very concerned about the family. When I look back I realize the manner I raised my boy was exactly like I was raised. Now he has two little boys. My son is doing the same thing with his little boys as happened in his young life. We visited the church where he was serving as the executive pastor and when we arrived we found him at the front door greeting the people as they arrived. Standing beside him was his four-year-old, putting his little hand up, greeting the people alongside his father.

I wrote earlier about how my father would take me calling on people every day when he was a pioneer preacher. I thought that was what you were supposed to do. When my boy was a pre-schooler I would go by my home in the afternoon and pick him up and take him with me to the rest homes.

When Jeff came home from college, he knew that we would spend the one day visiting in the rest homes together. He would come to my office at eleven in the morning and we would take the rest of the day visiting people. We would drive 100 miles that day around the community making all of our stops. I would say to those elderly people, "Jeff came home from college and wanted to see you." Many of them couldn't remember that he visited them before, or who he was, or even that I had been there last week. He was great with them. Some of the elderly ladies would take his face in their hands. They would rub his face and tell him that he was pretty. You know that no boys are "pretty", but he would sit there and let them touch him.

One Christmas we spent Christmas Eve in his home. When we arrived no one was there. We had a key to his house and let ourselves in. It got later and later. We knew his wife was working late that night, but wondered where Jeff might be. When he finally arrived, we inquired what had brought him home so late. He said, "I've been at the rest homes." I replied, "That's not in your portfolio of ministry." He said, "I know, but it's Christmas and nobody else was going." That made this father feel good.

We pick up these things from our parents. That is the tragedy of today. Many children are growing up among us with no one to model after.

I performed a wedding for a young lady whose mother had been married ten times. I said to her, "I respect your mother, but you need a model. Please watch Nancy and me real close." I was unable to spend a great deal of time with her, but I asked her to please watch us. She had no model to help her be a wife and mother. That is what is happening in our world today. It breaks my heart when I see these little people growing up with no discipline, no example, and no model.

Nobody seems to care, and I am worried about what we are producing. That is why we need a loving church family to love people. We must be patient with these little people who come from some of these difficult backgrounds. We need people to come along side of them and encourage them.

The church has great opportunities today to support the family. We can provide a "family" for those who have been disenfranchised from the family and have gone through the pain of separation, desertion and divorce. With so many forces coming against the family we can be a support to those who are endeavoring to maintain strong relationships and produce spiritually and morally healthy children.

Every year as a pastor we would have a special seminar during the year for couples. We would take advantage of family days such as Mother's Day and Father's Day to have special emphasis on the home. It paid off. I can honestly say that in the twenty years I was in one pulpit I can count on one hand the members in that church who went through a divorce. There were people who were attendees and were on the fringe who went through some serious problems, but the actual members of that church were strong in their marital relationships and commitments.

We can't give up on the family. I recall conducting a funeral for a godly woman who had several grandchildren present who were not living as Christians. I reminded them how their grandmother had prayed for them and that now she would no longer be praying, but I was hoping her prayers would be answered. Some months later after one of the severe California earthquakes I called my friends, the son of the woman, and heard voices in the background. I was told their son was home visiting and that his life has been completely transformed by the power of God. I believe it was through the prayers of his grandmother.

My encouragement to you is... keep praying. God is interested in redeeming entire families.

Chapter Seventeen

A PRODUCTIVE CHURCH

This New Testament church was a productive church. They produced what they claimed.

Jess Moody has a wonderful book, titled, 'A Drink at Joel's Place." In that book he draws an analogy between "Joel's place", based on the prophecy of Joel in the Old Testament, and "Joe's Place", the local bar. I was inspired by the book to preach a sermon, "Where Are You Doing Your Drinking?"

Moody states in his book, "… a bar provides the intoxication it advertises. A bar is always true to its name. When a customer comes in, they don't inform him that the only thing they serve is warm milk. If they were to do this, as many barflies would stay away from Joe's Bar as church members stay away from Sunday worship." The bottom line is if the bar does not produce what it advertises it will go out of business in a very short time. I think that if the church of Jesus is not going to produce what it advertises then let's closes the doors.[7]

While I was serving as a college president I became acquainted with a student from Alaska. She was a woman in her mid-forties. Lydia told me a fascinating story of her background. She was a recovered alcoholic. Alcohol was part of her life in her developing years. She said that when she was a little girl she would walk by the bars and hear all the laughter and frivolity, and would say to herself, "As soon as I get old enough I am going there." She did. On the day of her legal-age birthday she went to the bar. That day was the beginning of her alcoholism. When she told me that story, I said, "Lydia, that's what should have happened when you walked by the church. You should have heard, and seen, all of those happy people and a desire should have been created in you to be part of that kind of fellowship. Your past life was not all your fault, it was the fault of the church for not presenting to you a happy, wholesome, positive image."

The questions we need to ask, drawn from the analogy of Joel's Place and Joe's Bar, are ... "Is there a better fellowship at church than there is down at the corner bar? Can you come into this atmosphere and be as honest with people as you can down at the bar? Can you crawl up on the stool here at the church (known as the pew) and pour your heart out to somebody as easy as you can down at the bar? Can you share your needs with people at church and know that your confidence will not be betrayed and that somebody will cry with you and feel what you feel?

The bar advertises that if you go down there you can get intoxicated. When the bar starts serving drinks that won't get people intoxicated, nobody will want to go to them. That is what they advertise! We advertise that if you come to church you can have a life-changing experience with God. We advertise that you will find a better fellowship than you will find in any place in the world. This New Testament church produced what they advertised. It is up to us to see that what we advertise is what we produce.

This kind of a church will produce growth. A powerful twenty-first century church that is alive is going to be a growing church. There may be exceptions if you live in a small town and they close down the only industry in town. But in the majority of places there are people moving in and people in the community who do not go to any church.

There is a law of life that says, "If you are not growing you are dying." A tree puts on a new ring of growth every year. When it ceases to do that it is dead. It may stand for awhile. It may look like a tree. It may even put on some needles and foliage. But one day a storm will come. We've seen it happen many times in the Northwest part of our country. When the big winds come and those giant fir trees begin to fall, you often discover that the trees were dead on the inside. Decay had begun because they had stopped growing. There were still branches, there was bark on the outside, but inside they were dead. They looked alive, but had been dead for some time.

That's the same principle in a church. If we are not adding rings of growth, we can look like a church, we can act like a church, we can call ourselves a church, but we are dead on the inside if there is not new life occurring. One day the doors of that church will close for the final time and it will all be over.

That New Testament church was a productive church. Miracles were occurring. Lives were being changed. Society was being affected.

Chapter Eighteen

A POSSIBILITY THINKING CHURCH

This church was constantly living in a spirit of optimism where possibilities became a reality.

They saw the glorious potential all around them. They must have received this spirit from their Master because He picked a bunch of "no names", losers, and made winners out of them.

In our recruitment of college students I was always pleased to see those bright, high achievers with strong grade point averages and strong leadership qualities. However, we cannot overlook someone who we think might not have all the desirable qualifications. We need to look beyond the current perception to the possibilities that may lay dormant in someone.

Shortly after assuming my responsibilities as president of Northwest College, a young man who had recently graduated from the college came to see me. He is part native-American. He is an extremely handsome person. When he entered my office he said, "I came to meet you and to thank you for this college. I was an abused child all of my early life. I was beaten and always told that I was dumb and that I was a loser. I didn't do well in school. I came to this college. One day a professor came to me and said, 'You don't know how to read, do you?' I confessed to Him that I didn't." He went on to say that no one had ever taken the time to discover that he was dyslexic. This professor took him under his wing and tutored him. He graduated from college. He said to me, "You don't know what it is like to get up in the pulpit and be able to read the Bible." He is a brilliant young man. He is doing great things for God. Here was someone who had been classified a loser until a professor saw possibilities in him.

I went to the professor and told him the story. Here is what surprised me. The professor didn't remember doing it, which tells me he was doing it for a lot of other people.

Those are the kind of people Jesus loved. People nobody wanted. People who had been beaten up in life. People who thought they could never change. He saw the possibilities in their lives and said, "You don't have to be what you are. You can be something different." He lifted them up and caused them to believe in the power and potential that was in their lives, and they became something.

I love the story of Zacchaeus. Nobody liked him. Who likes a tax collector? He was hated. Jesus, as He was passing through Jericho that day was at the zenith of his popularity. He could have dined with the mayor or with a senator. He could have eaten with anybody. Everybody wanted to be with Him. But He looked up in a tree and said to a man that was handicapped by his physical size and his profession, "I want to eat at your house." He went home with Zacchaeus and the Bible says, "That day Zacchaeus and his entire house believed." Jesus said, "You are my kind of guy! I like you!" The religious people hated Him. Jesus often picked people nobody else would pick. They said he was always hanging out with sinners. His response to them was, " 'I didn't come to save the righteous. I came to save those who are lost." He saw the possibilities.

When you are a person of possibilities, you are a person of great vision and faith. You see things other people don't see. You are willing to pay a price others don't pay because you see the potential and possibilities ahead of you. The possibilities are worth the pain. Sure, you are going to have disappointments. You are going to invest in individuals who will turn their back on you. After helping people they may become critical and forsake you.

But, there are those whose lives are totally turned around and become productive citizens, strong leaders of their families, and solid Christians. It is worth believing for the best.

Chapter Nineteen

A PROTECTED CHURCH

I believe that when you are moving in God's will, God in some way will put a wall around you to keep you. I'm not implying that there will never be difficulties and problems, or that this life will be pain free.

You can be in the center of God's will and suffer pain. One of my most encouraging passages of scripture, especially when I am going through difficult times in the place where I am certain God has called me, is the account when Jesus told His disciples to go to the other side of the lake. This was not just a suggestion. The King James Version uses the word, "constrained." "He constrained them to the other side." This was an audible directive from Jesus Himself. In the midst of the following of His instructions they ran into a "head wind." Wouldn't it be reasonable to believe that if you are in the will of God and in perfect obedience to God that you would avoid the "head winds"? It seems as if you should have tail winds, or at least those soft side winds to fill the sails.

These people in the New Testament church lived in the protective presence of God. Even when they were being dragged behind Roman chariots, fed to lions, taken to the guillotine, there was a sense of the protection of God around their souls and they knew God was with them. There is nothing that will ever come to you and me that our God doesn't know about. God will give us the grace and strength for that situation and for that day.

That spirit of protection was manifested in their lives toward others who were part of that fellowship. Their motivation for organization was to care for the widows. They expressed God's protection to those who were not able to provide and protect themselves.

Let me digress for just a moment. I have not talked about the organization of this church. We must not overlook the fact that this was a highly organized church. They did not organize just for the sake of organization. They organized to meet a need. If you do any kind of serious calculations you could easily ascertain that this early church may have grown to 100,000 members and didn't even have deacons.

James, the half-brother of Jesus, was the pastor of the church in Jerusalem. I hear people talking about who they want to meet in heaven and the conversations they want to have. I want to meet Pastor James. I want to talk to him about his organizational skills. I want to know how he kept this exploding church organized and moving in the proper direction. No wonder we don't have a lot of letters from James in the New Testament. He was too busy to write letters. He was leading this dynamic church.

Finally, the workload became so heavy that they appointed deacons. The deacons were not living under the call from God to the unique ministry of a pastor. They were appointed by the church so the pastors would have more time for study, prayer and preparation.

Spiritual headship and leadership in the church always flows through the pastor, not through the board. It flows through the pastor and is carried out by those appointed to assist in the practical aspects of the ministry. These men were appointed by the church to carry on the physical functions of the church. That is the New Testament pattern.

That church had phenomenal growth and influence while they lived under the divine protection of the Lord. He surrounded them with His protection. When a church follows spiritual principles, they will have spiritual protection. God has a great love for the church, so much so that He gave His Son to die, and to be resurrected as the head of the church.

Chapter Twenty

A PATIENT CHURCH

Patience is a difficult principle to practice. The ability to wait is difficult. I must have a problem. One day in my inter-office mail box someone had placed a plaque with these words … "Oh God, Grant Me Patience, But Hurry!" That's the way we are. "God, we want patience, but hurry!"

This principle was illustrated in the upper room when the followers of Jesus were told to wait. They didn't know exactly what they were waiting for, but they were just told to wait for the promised Holy Spirit. This was a patient church. You will find that same Spirit all through the Book of Acts. Those people had the ability to wait on God.

There are two tragedies in the life of a church. One is to get ahead of God. The other is to fail to catch the wave of God's blessing when it goes by and miss God's plan. The "wave" doesn't come by all the time. We need to recognize those seasons of God's blessings in a church and in our individual lives. Then we need the courage and boldness to move out when God begins to work.

I like action. I don't like processing. I don't like waiting. But, I believe that a God-given idea can be processed. It can go through the crucible of testing and come out on the other side. A good idea often needs to be refined and this is accomplished by waiting.

I referred to it an earlier chapter and wish I had the space to share more of the agony and the heartache I went through from the time our congregation voted to relocate the church until the time we finally got it done. It was through a waiting time that evaluations were made and plans readjusted that saved the work of God thousands of dollars. I learned many lessons during those months. One I learned is that God always comes up with the right answer at the right time.

I have seen how some people want to act so quickly during times of church discipline. They want to bring judgment on someone now. I think we need to wait and let God work through some situations. That same principle of waiting applies to our families and our businesses. Time has a wonderful way of leading us to the right answers and preventing big mistakes.

I had an aunt who served as a Justice of the Peace. She would perform up to twenty-three weddings a day. She also dealt with divorce cases. She told me that she would never let anyone file for divorce on the day they came in to file. She always told them to come back the next day. She said, "I have had women come who no doubt needed help. I saw them with black eyes and knew they had been beaten up. I knew that in the heat of their problem they wanted to file for divorce." She told them, "Come back tomorrow." She was amazed how many did not come back. You see, time has a way of healing things.

We need to come to that place of absolute trust and confidence where we can wait on God. I've seen individuals, churches, and organizations fail to wait and then find themselves in great difficulties. I believe that when we wait for God's timing and find God's will and His direction, then He is going to send the resources and people to get the job done. God is looking at our hearts. When He finds our motives right and knows we are moving in the direction that will honor Him, then He will send what we need to get the job done.

Often in my experience we didn't have the resources, the expertise, or the people. But when we were in the place where God wanted us to be, doing what He wanted to have done, we saw the people and the resources there to accomplish it. It takes patience to wait on God.

One night in a church board meeting we were dealing with a discipline problem in the church. The board wanted to excommunicate a person in the church because they were causing dissension. They wanted to go immediately from the board meeting and deal with this person. I said, "No, we're not going to do that. We're going to pray." Within hours, the judgment of God fell on that person and the whole church knew it. We could have gone over there and messed the whole situation up and caused all kinds of confusion. Through our willingness to wait, God used this to bring growth to the church and a new respect for Him and the leadership He had placed in the church.

God takes care of difficult situations if we can just have the patience to wait on Him. That was the spirit of this New Testament church. They had learned to wait.

Chapter Twenty-One

A PEACEFUL CHURCH

===

"Then had the churches rest throughout all Judea and Galilee and Samaria, and were edified: and walking in the fear of the Lord, and in the comfort of the Holy Ghost, were multiplied" (Acts 9:31 KJV).

I used the King James Version for only one purpose. We read that "the churches had rest" ... and "were multiplied." Some might be tempted to interpret that word "rest" for inactivity. That in no way was the attitude of this church. Nearly every other translation of this verse uses the word "peace" ... *"the church had a time of peace"* (Today's English Version) ... *"the church enjoyed a time of peace"* (NIV) ... *"the church was left in peace"* (New English Bible) ... *"The whole Church now enjoyed a period of peace"* (Phillips Modern English).

This is a marvelous verse with which to end these "Twenty-One Positive Principles for a Powerful Twenty-First Century Church." Without peace no church will grow. I am aware that I am taking this word "peace" out of context. The reference in the New Testament was that they had now entered into a time when persecution against the church had ceased.

However, I do not believe there will be sustained, spiritual growth in a church unless there is a spirit of peace. We will never see revival, renewal, or growth in the church without peace.

God is quite concerned where He puts His spiritual babies. He will not put them into a place of confusion and unrest. They tell us that even an infant can sense what is going on in a home. If there is strife and bickering in the home, a little baby senses that. Sometimes they become sick because of the tension and strife they feel. That is one reason I have always welcomed babies into the church. I love to see them being held in the arms of loving parents during the worship experience. I know we need to have nurseries today, and it is convenient for parents to have well supervised facilities and staff to care for their children. I do believe that there is something in the very atmosphere in a place where God is honored that can minister to the spirit of a little child.

A church has to contend for peace. There must be a commitment from leadership that is expressed throughout the entire church, that this a place of peace. I went for twenty consecutive years without ever having a dissenting vote on the Board of Deacons. That took some give and take, but this group of people was committed to unity and harmony in the church. That commitment by the leadership was expressed to the entire congregation and we never had disharmony. That was not artificial; it was a life-style that came out of dedication to God.

Once I had one of our deacons come to me regarding a rather personal thing that had happened; a decision that I had made that had affected him personally. He followed me out of a board meeting one night, put his arm around me and said, "I don't understand or agree with everything you've done, but I want you to know this … I support you." Rather than defend myself and defend the decision I had made, I just gave him a hug and said, "I really appreciate that and I love you."

One of the marks of this New Testament Church was that "they were all in one accord."

Bitterness is a terrible thing. We have all been hurt by someone. We have the choice of what we are going to do with our hurts and misunderstandings. I've hurt people. I've done and said things that were misinterpreted, sometimes through ignorance and other times through carelessness. I have also been hurt by the actions of others. However, I have made a decision that relates to me. I will not carry those hurts around.

I was involved in a church problem that needed my attention as a District Superintendent. I met with the members and did the best I knew how. Years later I met a man from that church. He told me we had met before and reminded me where. On the verge of tears he said to me, "I need to ask your forgiveness." I responded that I knew of nothing that needed to be forgiven. He said, "I have held bad feelings in my heart toward you for the way you handled that situation." I replied, "I never knew that. I have no lingering bad feelings over what transpired." He said, "I know that. I'm the one that needs to be forgiven. I must get this bitterness out of my heart." That was a very positive thing he did. Generally, bitterness in a person's heart does not affect the person to whom the bitterness is directed, but has devastating affects on the person filled with bitterness. This kind of attitude will affect the emotional, physical and spiritual health. Life is too short to let these kind of events become such a focal factor that it destroys us.

I have a cousin who was a funeral director for many years. He had taken care of the funeral arrangements for a deceased man whose remains were to be cremated. His wife asked if she could observe the cremation. He told her that this was highly out of the ordinary. But, she insisted, "I want to do it." He said to her, "I don't recommend that." She asked, "Can you stop me?" He told her, "No, I guess I can't stop you." So they placed the remains in the incinerator. She walked up to the door, looked through the window and said, "I hope that is hot enough for you, you son-of-a-gun."

All that bitterness! What a way to live! I don't think her bitterness got consumed in the flames because bitterness goes deeper than that. Who wants to live like that? We can let a little seed of bitterness come and it grows into an orchard that consumes us.

While I was living in Salem, Oregon, the Superintendent of the State Police was assassinated one morning on the steps of the State Capital. Years before he had been the county sheriff of one of the Metro Portland counties. He had fired a deputy sheriff. This man left and established a cleaning business and was quite successful. But the bitterness over that firing never got out of his heart and it continued to grow. One morning, as Holly Holcomb was leaving the State Capital, this man stepped out from behind a bush and shot him. He died instantly.

I would often visit in the Holly Holcomb maternity ward at Salem Memorial Hospital. Every time I went there to see new babies and their proud parents, I thought about Holly Holcomb and was also reminded what bitterness could do to a person…how it can absolutely destroy you.

There are times when a leader must take a strong stand if for nothing more than to insure that unity is maintained in a church. Often I would say from the pulpit, "We have unity in this church. There is not a devil within the confines of this building, because he cannot work where there is unity. We will not permit him to work here as we are going to dedicate ourselves to peace and unity." No one wanted to move away from that kind of spirit. Those kind of statements help to produce a spirit where people continue to work together in unity.

The witness of that kind of church to an unbelieving world is a powerful thing. The mark of the New Testament church was that they loved each other. The Word declares, "By this shall all men know that you are my disciples, that you love one another."

All of these previous principles are totally negated if we do not have love. All of these other things shall pass away, but love never fails. The Living Bible states in I Corinthians 13:13, *"There are three things that remain—faith, hope, and love—and the greatest of these is love."* So, let's love! Let's love our God. Let's love each other. Let's love Christ's church. Let's love the lost. Let's love the unlovely. Let's love the difficult person. Let's love....

After having shared with you these principles I have practiced and observed, let me offer a prayer for you who are endeavoring to be all that Christ wants you to be in this world.

Dear God of all grace and power, we humbly present ourselves to you asking for your help that we will always be people who ...possess a heart that is sensitive to our own sin ...keep sticking with our task when others around us quit ...seek the strength that comes by working with others ... tap into prayer power, our greatest resource ...study to show ourselves worthy representatives of your Word ... preach with a life that backs up our message ... develop people around us to use their gifting and talents ... are faithful and examples in our financial stewardship ... find and live within the purpose you have for us ... keep ourselves pure in our morals and relationships ... stand for right even though it may cost us our lives ... praise You in the midst of our personal problems ... experience the power available for us on a daily basis ... are not fearful of being change agents when needed ... seek your help that your will be accomplished in our families ... are all that we claim to be... see the limitless possibilities all around us ... recognize that we are surrounded by your protection ... learn to wait for the wave of your blessing and not to miss it ... live in peace and unity to see you kingdom advanced.

We thank you for hearing our prayer that we offer in the Name of Him Who loved the church and gave His life for it, even Jesus Christ, the Chief Cornerstone, our Savior. AMEN

ENDNOTES

[1] Thomas E. Trask, Wayde I. Goodall, and Zenas J. Bicket, *The Pentecostal Pastor* (Springfield, Missouri: Gospel Publishing House 1997)

[2] Robert H. Schuller, *Your Church Has a Fantastic Future*, (Glendale, California, Regal Books, A Division) of Gospel Light Publications, 1986

[3] C. Peter Wagner, *Your Spiritual Gifts Can Help Your Church Grow* (Glendale, California: Regal Books Division, A Divison of Gospel Light Publications 1979)

[4] Jim Cymbala, *Fresh Wind, Fresh Fire* (Grand Rapids, Michigan: Zondervan Publishing House, 1997)

[5] Cliff C. Jones, *Winning Through Integrity* (Nashville Tennessee: Abingdon Press 1985)

[6] Merlin R. Carothers, *Prison to Praise* (London, England: Hodder & Stoughton 1966)

[7] Jess Moody, *A Drink At Joel's Place* (Waco, Texas: Word Publishers 1967)

Printed in the United States
133846LV00001B/97-219/A

9 781591 603153